STARCRAFT™

Expansion Set: Brood War™
Prima's Official Strategy Guide

Bart Farkas

PRIMA PUBLISHING
Rocklin, California
(916) 632-4400
www.primagames.com

Project Editor: Sara E. Wilson

ISBN: 7615-1811-8
Library of Congress Catalog Card Number: 98-67344
Printed in the United States of America

01 JJ 2524

DEDICATION

For Cori (Push!)

ACKNOWLEDGMENTS

Many people at Blizzard deserve a huge thank you for their efforts. First, thanks must go out to Shane Dibiri, Chris Sigaty, Mike Morhaime, and especially Bill Roper (for pulling it all together and assembling all the resources I needed to make this book happen). For John Lagrave, Eric Dodds, and Scott Mercer, I owe a serious debt of gratitude for their intergral help in solving several of *Brood War*'s challenges. My thanks go out, as well, to the rest of the staff at Blizzard for their tips, strategies, insights and general, all-round help during this process. I'd especially like to single out Derek Simmons, Brian Love, and Frank Gilson for their contributions.

From Prima, thanks also must go out to Sara Wilson and Amy Raynor. Finally, thanks to Jeff Govier for his help with the early Zerg missions. Jeff is a true scholar and a gentleman.

Contents

How to Use This Book

When I was working on the strategy guide for the original *Starcraft*™ game, it was obvious to me the game I was playing in beta form would become a monster hit, and, without a doubt, *Starcraft* was *the* game to own in 1998. It has all the elements—jaw-dropping cinematic sequences, great graphics, and gameplay so addictive I could play through the entire night without realizing it! My only clue to the time was the few threads of sunlight coming in through the curtains. Even then, it was hard to stop playing before I was satisfied I'd put the Zerg in their place.

Starcraft™: Brood War™ takes perhaps the best computer game of all time and (almost unbelievably) improves on it. With several new kick-butt cinematics and six new units, *Brood War* will exceed the expectations of gaming fans, whether they've played the original *Starcraft* or are new to the Starcraft universe. *Starcraft* succeeds because, although it's easy to learn, it's amazingly complex when it comes to mounting successful strategies. I find it a constant source of amazement in how many unique strategies and opinions a single *Starcraft* or *Brood War* mission can elicit from a group of gamers. Of five gamers playing the same level, you can end up with five different opinions on how to win.

If it were possible to bottle this magic, then every game ever made could be this great. But it's not—and thank goodness. *Starcraft: Brood War* is one of those rare computer games that brings all gaming elements together in a symphony of excellence.

Because *Brood War* is an expansion set, you can expect another layer (or two) of difficulty in many missions. This guide exists to help you through the sticky parts.

Strategy

It's safe to assume you'll find ways to defeat a scenario that differ from the strategies provided in these pages, and that's OK. If you follow this book's guidance for each scenario, you'll win, but this guidance is *not* the be-all and end-all. Rather, it's distilled from tried-and-true methods of defeating every mission.

I recommend you attempt to defeat each scenario by yourself first—give it at least a couple of tries—before seeking this book's strategies. Finding your own ways to defeat the tougher *Brood War* levels is well worth the effort. If frustration sets in, however, this book is here to get you through.

Chapter 2, the background information chapter, is chock-full of strategies and tips for each unit type in all species. This chapter will serve you well and I recommend you read it all.

Use Chapter 2 and Chapter 3 together to meld individual unit strategies in the former with the latter's overall tips and strategies. Many of the tips and tricks in Chapter 3 came straight from the fine folks at the Blizzard testing department, giving you access to the world's most experienced *Starcraft* gamers. Their advice will serve you well.

Chapters 4, 5, and 6 provide detailed strategies for defeating each scenario. Refer to this section when you really need help. Reading up on strategy before you begin a mission takes away some of *Starcraft: Brood War*'s magic. Don't use it as a walkthrough. Instead, use the mission strategies when you're really stuck or after you've finished a mission successfully. You'll be surprised how often your strategy differs from the ones in this book—proof of *Starcraft*'s wonderful complexity.

Chapter 7 will give you a hand with setting up a multiplayer game, and provides strategies and tips for surviving in the cutthroat world of mano a mano and group *Starcraft* gaming. Multiplayer action is where *Starcraft*'s (and now the expansion pack's) legacy truly will live on. If you love the game as much as most players, you'll be eager to get online and acquire the skills you need to succeed in the Battle.net™ realm.

As with the original *Starcraft*, the folks at Blizzard have included a Campaign Editor on the *Starcraft* CD. This handy tool allows you to create your own entirely new *Starcraft* campaigns, complete with everything but cinematics. I grabbed a couple of Blizzard employees to help me walk you through the basic process of scenario designing and furnish you with a staring point.

The appendices provide detailed tables with gobs of statistical information for each unit and structure. A "counter table" supplies a reasonable opposing counterpart from each of the other two species. For example, what Zerg unit best counters the Marine? This information may seem mundane, but once you've mastered the nuances of the Starcraft realm, you'll find knowing even the smallest details can give you an edge. You'll also find those wonderful little cheat codes there to help you out when you get stuck.

In the end, you should take as much as you require from this book. Scan the tables, read up on unit strategies, or peruse the walkthroughs when you get frustrated. Take whatever you need to get the most out of *Starcraft: Brood War*. Enjoy.

TIP

Yes, Virginia, there is a **secret level**. Check out the end of Chapter 6 to learn how to access (and defeat) it.

The Units (and How to Use Them)

In this chapter you'll find statistics for each unit, as well as information that will help you understand each unit's strengths and weaknesses and how the units relate as you progress through the game. The tables in Appendix A supply further details, including ground and air attack values and unit counters for each species.

The Terran Force

The Terrans should hold a special place in your heart, if only because they're our humanoid cousins. If you play the game through from start to finish, your first 10 missions will be Terran-controlled and will give you a solid understanding of the mechanics and strategies you need to survive in *Starcraft*. For this reason, you should play from start to finish—Terrans first, then Zerg, and finally Protoss.

Terran units are no less potent than those of the other two species. Indeed, many game testers at Blizzard prefer the Terrans, with their cloaked Wraiths and mammoth Battlecruisers packing Yamato Cannons. Handled properly, the Terrans are a formidable force.

Ground Units

These units will fight your enemies on their own turf, paving the way to victory with your opponents' blood. You may be tempted to spend resources building flashy spaceships, but sometimes a group of inexpensive Marines can serve just as well. The addition of the Medic gives you all the more reason to rely on these ground units as your backbone.

MARINE

Armor: Light
Hit Points: 40
Ground Attack: 6
Air Attack: 6
Attack Range: 4
Gas Required: 0
Minerals Required: 50

The Marine is your bread-and-butter unit. Equally effective against both air and ground attacks, this versatile unit has decided many missions. Marines often back up Wraiths or Battlecruisers because of their powerful ability to mop up nagging ground-based air defense systems as their airborne counterparts clean out the skies.

TIP

If you need to get slightly better performance out of your Marines or firebats, use a Stimpack. The only disadvantage to this is that your unit loses some help.

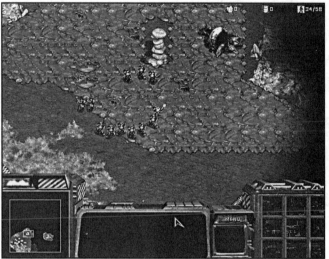

Fig. 2-1. The Terrans' most versatile units, Marines can rock-and-roll both on the ground and against airborne enemies.

Groups of Marines can use their rifles to take down small and medium-sized squadrons of light airships quickly. Consider the Marine an alternative to the Missile Turret whenever building one is prohibitive. Using Marines as mobile "Missile Turrets," you can deal a heavy blow to ground and air units alike, but remember, they must travel in groups of eight or more.

Fig. 2-2. Defensive Marines in Bunkers are difficult to beat.

7

Although Marines can take a decent fight to enemy units, they really shine on the ground, stacked by fours in a Bunker. This is especially true in the Zerg levels, where Terran bases are hit with wave after wave of Zerglings and Hydralisks. A Bunker full of Marines with extended range and beefed-up attack values can mow down small groups of enemies indefinitely. A grid of Bunkers is virtually impenetrable.

FIREBAT

Armor: Light
Hit Points: 50
Ground Attack: 16*
Air Attack: 0
Attack Range: 2
Gas Required: 25
Minerals Required: 50

Their limited range and lack of an air attack give Firebats a more defined role than the Marines'. Firebats cost more, as well (requiring Vespene). But they have value in many Terran missions, and can be instrumental in winning several battles against the Zerg.

Fig. 2-3. Firebats and Zerglings—a good combination if you're Terran.

The Firebat is essentially a flamethrower, with a threefold attack advantage over the Marine. This can be deceptive, however, because attacking heavy armor can lower the Firebat's attack value by 75 percent. An attack value of 16 doesn't look so good reduced to 4.

*Attack value limited against some units (see Appendix A).

The answer? Use the Firebat when you can best exploit its weapons.

Firebats are very effective against Zergling hordes, particularly from the protection of a Bunker. A combination of Marines (for attack range) and Firebats (for raw power) in a series of defensive Bunkers will smoke Zerglings and Hydralisks. Terran Mission 1, "First Strike" is an excellent opportunity to demonstrate this.

Firebat groups are also excellent for destroying enemy buildings and structures. A posse of eight Firebats circling an enemy building will incinerate it in seconds. A popular strategy (see Mission 1, "First Strike") is to use equal groups of Firebats and Marines (and a few Medics) as a one-two punch against enemy forces. Firebats are also very effective against Protoss Zealots units, because they must attack hand-to-hand and are vulnerable to fire due to their light armor.

Fig. 2-4. This Firebat/Marine circling technique works well in the early Terran missions.

Firebat groups also are excellent for destroying enemy buildings/structures. A posse of eight to 12 Firebats circling an enemy building will incinerate it in seconds. A popular strategy is to use equal groups of Firebats and Marines as a one–two punch against enemy forces (see Terran Mission 6, "Emperor's Flight"). Firebats also are very effective against Protoss Zealots, because those lightly armored units must attack hand-to-hand and are vulnerable to fire.

MEDIC

Armor: Light
Hit Points: 60
Ground Attack: 0
Air Attack: 0
Attack Range: 0
Gas Required: 25
Minerals Required: 50

The Medic is another unit new to *Brood War*, with far-reaching implications for troop-management. Medics not only heal your troops when you order them to do so, they'll even do this automatically, if they're close enough to injured units. Keeping a pair of Medics in a group of 10 Marines is a great way to keep everyone healthy and happy.

Although Healing is the Medic's base ability, this unit can obtain another pair of abilities—Restoration and Optic Flare.

Restoration removes almost any effect afflicting a unit, including Parasite, Plague, Lockdown, and Irradiate. Obviously, you'll benefit from having a Medic handy when a Defiler hits your expensive Battlecruisers with Plague. Research Restoration as soon as it becomes available.

Fig. 2-5. A couple of Medics can go a long way toward healing a squad of Marines.

Although the Medic can't actually attack, you *can* research his Optical Flare ability. Optical Flare blinds the affected unit so it can only see a very short distance (one matrix square). The best part is that it's permanent; after a unit is subjected to the Flare, it's sight will always be short, which makes

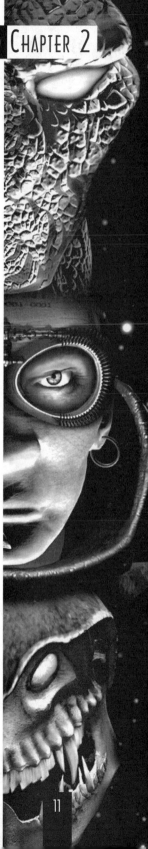

getting around lone Siege Tanks a breeze. A blinded unit still can fire on you, however, if there's a unit nearby to spot for it, so use it against lone units. If you expose detector units, such as Overlords or Observers, to an Optical Flare, they won't be detecting anything anymore.

GHOST

Armor: Light
Hit Points: 45
Ground Attack: 10*
Air Attack: 10*
Attack Range: 6
Gas Required: 75
Minerals Required: 25

Given its light armor, relatively low hit points, and unique skills, you'll rarely produce the Ghost in bulk. However, it's one of the game's most important units, especially if you're fond of nuclear weaponry.

The Ghost's most versatile feature is its Cloak; usually you must research it to gain access to it. The Cloak special ability renders the Ghost "invisible" to most enemy units, leaving it free to wander deep into enemy territory to scout or paint a target for a Nuke. The Cloak isn't without drawbacks, however: detector units, such as Observers and Missile Turrets, can spot cloaked Ghosts and enable other units to open fire on them.

Fig. 2-6. The cloaked Ghost is a powerful tool if you use caution around detector units.

* Attack value limited against some units (see Appendix A).

Lockdown is another ability unique to the Ghost. This special missile temporarily immobilizes mechanized units. This comes in handy if an enemy Siege Tank or Battlecruiser is giving your base trouble; just "lock it down" and take it out. Of course, this does little good against the Zerg, but you'll have plenty of opportunities to use Lockdown in the course of playing *Starcraft: Brood War*.

The Ghost's last, best feature is its ability to "paint" an enemy target for a nuclear strike. Once the target is painted, a red laser-sighting dot displays, and after about 10 seconds, the Nuke will drop. *Boom*. The Ghost is the only unit that can do this; sadly, it's often lost in the blast. The resulting damage is worth it, however. A Nuke will do substantial (if not terminal) damage to all units and structures within a large radius.

Fig. 2-7. When a Nuke goes off, you'll know it.

GOLIATH

Armor: Heavy

Hit Points: 125

Ground Attack: 12

Air Attack: 20*

Attack Range: 5

Gas Required: 50

Minerals Required: 100

* Attack value limited against some units (see Appendix A).

The Goliath is the cream of your infantry, striking fear in the hearts of the enemy. The Goliath's powerful ground attack and even more devastating air defense system are impressive. En masse, Goliaths can knock any enemy unit from the sky in seconds and are as formidable as Marines on the ground.

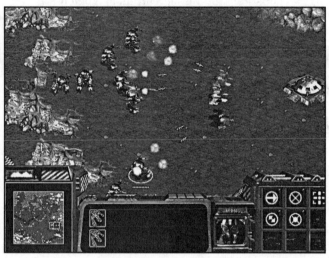

Fig. 2-8. The Goliath's ability to take out air units is perhaps its greatest advantage.

Goliaths can provide ground support for Marines or Firebats; more importantly, they provide a high-powered air defense system—25 percent more potent than the Wraith's air-to-air attack! Twelve Marines backed up with four to six Goliaths are a force to reckon with when they advance on enemy positions.

Fig. 2-9. Surprisingly, Zerglings can pose a bit of a problem for an isolated Goliath.

The Goliath's bulk renders it vulnerable to attacks by swarming enemies, such as Zerglings. One or two Goliaths against a group of 10 Zerglings are in trouble. When you can, protect your units by grouping two kinds together, such as Firebats and Marines, or Marines and Goliaths. New to *Brood War* is the Goliath's Charon Boosters missile upgrade; take advantage of it as soon as you can. With this upgrade your Goliaths can substitute for Missile Turrets in a pinch.

SCV

Armor: Light
Hit Points: 60
Ground Attack: 5
Air Attack: 0
Attack Range: 1
Gas Required: 0
Minerals Required: 50

The SCV looks like it might make a good fighting unit. However, it doesn't really mix it up well. Use this unit for combat only in emergency situations. Having the SCV harvest gas and minerals is a far more efficient use of the resources it took to build the unit.

Fig. 2-10. SCVs are for building structures and harvesting resources. Try not to get into this situation.

If it happens that SCVs are your base's only line of defense, group them and throw them at the enemy en masse. This might be your only chance until you can build more effective fighting units.

Keep an SCV hanging around just behind the front lines, so it can scoot in and repair damaged Goliaths or Siege Tanks (or even air units) when the going gets tough. Bringing a damaged unit back from the brink with an SCV is a lot cheaper than building another.

SIEGE TANK

Armor: Heavy

Hit Points: 150

Ground Attack (Tank): 30*

Ground Attack (Siege): 70*

Air Attack: 0

Attack Range (Siege): 12

Attack Range (Tank): 6

Gas Required : 100

Minerals Required: 150

The ability to convert to Siege mode and fire high-powered shells farther than any other unit in the game makes the Siege Tank perhaps the Terrans' most popular (and awesome) unit. However, the Siege Tank is vulnerable to air attacks and attacks by large numbers of ground units.

Fig. 2-11. As a tank, this unit deals good damage, but it really shines in a different mode.

The Siege Tank offers a good combination of mobility and firepower in combat situations. In fact, when your troops are moving so fast you don't bother to pause to regroup, leaving your Siege Tanks in Tank mode is probably a good idea. Otherwise they can fall behind the protective envelope of your supporting troops and become open to attack.

15

* Attack value limited against some units (see Appendix A).

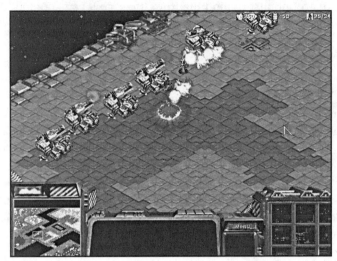

Fig. 2-12. Siege mode rules. A row of Siege Tanks can lay waste to vast numbers of advancing enemy units. Used in conjunction with a Bunker, they're dynamite.

After you research Siege mode, your tank strategy changes dramatically. The Siege Tank has an explosive attack strength of 70 and a range of 12 (the game's highest). The combined values provide exceptional power you can use to level enemy bases in minutes. By moving up your forces in groups of Marines, Wraiths, and Siege Tanks (in Siege mode), with each group of units protecting the others, you can advance on the enemy at will.

Siege Tanks in Siege mode can't move! And they have minimal range, so they're vulnerable to close-in attacks.

Vulture

Armor: Medium
Hit Points: 80
Ground Attack: 20*
Air Attack: 0
Attack Range: 5
Gas Required: 0
Minerals Required: 75

The Vulture is a hovercycle that's fast, powerful, and very effective when quick response time is critical. It holds a special place in *Starcraft*, because it's the vehicle of choice for Jim Raynor, a main character. His Vulture, however, is a souped-up version of the normal craft, and not representative of the Vulture as a unit.

* Attack value limited against some units (see Appendix A).

Fig. 2-13. Raynor's Vulture isn't your typical unit. Remember that when you're ordering up a dozen ...

The Vulture uses Fragmentation Grenades as its primary weapon and, although they pack a decent punch, their effectiveness is diminished against heavily armored enemies. The Vulture's speed is its greatest asset; it can travel quickly from hot spot to hot spot in groups of three or four. This method of putting out fires can be very effective, especially when you're defending a sprawling base from intermittent attacks.

Fig. 2-14. A few carefully laid Spider Mines can provide both first-line defense and an early warning system.

The Vulture's special weapon is the Spider Mine. These little devices are very effective, both as defensive units and an early warning system. You must research Spider Mines, and even then you get only three mines per Vulture.

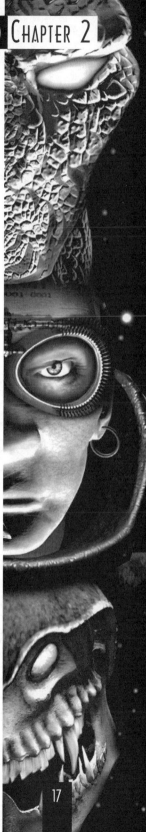

However, its power makes the Spider Mine worthwhile. When you set a Spider Mine, it burrows into the ground and waits for an enemy unit to get close. When it senses an enemy within its strike zone, it emerges and skitters toward the enemy. The resulting explosion usually will take out the enemy unit and severely damage any nearby.

MISSILE TURRET

Armor: Heavy
Hit Points: 200
Ground Attack: 0
Air Attack: 20*
Attack Range: 7
Gas Required: 0
Minerals Required: 100

There are two important things to remember about Missile Turrets:

    1. They're detectors, so they can spot cloaked enemy ships.
    2. They work much, much better in groups.

With that in mind, you should build your Missile Turrets in groups of at least three, and place one anywhere you're at risk from cloaked enemies.

Fig. 2-15. Turrets like to be grouped; otherwise they get lonely—and dead.

Keeping an SCV around to repair a damaged Missile Turret can save you rebuilding costs. Often the enemy will attack Missile Turrets in force one at a time, making them difficult to hang on to. But an SCV on the backside usually

* Attack value limited against some units (see Appendix A).

can repair the structure quickly and save it from destruction, while your other forces take care of the invaders.

Air Units

Terran air units are an impressive group featuring maneuverability, cloaking, high-powered weapons, and special abilities. These features make a dangerous combination, and with the new Valkyrie Frigate in your arsenal, you'll have a much easier time dominating the skies.

WRAITH
Armor: Heavy
Hit Points: 120
Ground Attack: 8
Air Attack: 20*
Attack Range: 5
Gas Required: 100
Minerals Required: 150

The Wraith is the Terrans' base air attack unit. Used in force, it offers a viable alternative to ground-based attacks. However, amassing a fleet of Wraiths can drain you quickly of the Vespene you need for other purposes. Try to ensure a solid Vespene supply before you build up a fleet.

Fig. 2-16. Wraiths are expensive, but nice to have.

19

* Attack value limited against some units (see Appendix A).

The Wraith may be a basic unit, but it has the impressive ability to cloak (when researched) in battle. Of course, cloaking is of little use near enemy detector units, such as Missile Turrets or Spore Colonies. But when the Wraith is hunting down enemy Transports or strafing advancing ground troops, it's usefulness is unsurpassed.

Fig. 2-17. Cloaked Wraiths can do some very serious damage to unsuspecting enemy units.

When assaulting an enemy position, the Wraith provides excellent air cover for Marines, Siege Tanks, and even Battlecruisers. If the enemy starts throwing air units at your strike force, cloak your Wraiths and take them out. Even if a nearby detector renders its Cloak ineffective, the Wraith's covering ability is second to none in the Terran forces.

Valkyrie Frigate

Armor: Medium
Hit Points: 200
Ground Attack: 0
Air Attack: 5 per missile*
Attack Range: 6
Gas Required: 125
Minerals Required: 250

The Frigate is the Terran equivalent of the Devourer. It's an air-to-air–only attacker, but its attack is very deadly, especially against groups of slow units, such as Overlords. The Valkyrie fires a salvo of eight missiles at once; each missile damages not only the unit it hits, but nearby units, as well. Three or four Valkyries grouped together can take out bunches of enemy units at once.

* Attack value limited against some units (see Appendix A).

TIP

Blizzard QA Testers suggest building Wraiths and Valkyries together. The Valkyries can eliminate airborne units while the Wraiths attack any ground units that come after your Valkyries.

Keep your Valkyries together in groups of three or more. If you can, it will take you a long way toward ruling the skies.

Fig. 2-18. Use Valkyries in groups of three or more to maximize their effectiveness.

BATTLECRUISER

Armor: Heavy
Hit Points: 500
Ground Attack: 25*
Air Attack: 25*
Air/Ground Attack (Yamato Cannon): 260*
Attack Range: 6
Attack Range (Yamato Cannon): 10
Gas Required: 300
Minerals Required: 400

If you're looking for an expensive unit, put the Battlecruiser at the top of the list. It's also possibly the Terrans' most powerful unit, so the cost can be worth it. The Battlecruiser is usually used as a primary weapon in a larger attack force, especially if it has the Yamato Cannon. It can meet an early demise if left unprotected against a group of enemy air units or a large group of Missile Turrets, so always keep a couple of protective Wraiths nearby.

21

* Attack value limited against some units (see Appendix A).

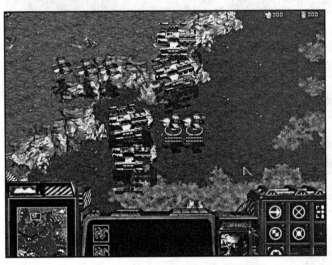

Fig. 2-19. Keep some backup near your Battlecruisers. They're worth protecting.

The Yamato Cannon is the Battlecruiser's special weapon. Grouped Battlecruisers' Yamato Cannons can take out an entire enemy base with just a few blasts. Say 10 Yamato-equipped Battlecruisers approach a Zerg base defended by five Spore Colonies. Five Battlecruisers use their Yamato Cannons to take out a Spore Colony with two shots, while the other five Battlecruisers hit the Hive with their Yamatos simultaneously. *Boom.* The Hive and the entire air defense network is gone in about 15 seconds.

Fig. 2-20. A bunch of Battlecruisers with enabled Yamato Cannons is an awesome destructive force.

Attacking with 10 Battlecruisers may sound like fun, but building the fleet requires huge amounts of resources. And while you pour your resources into Battlecruisers, your base is vulnerable to attack. If the enemy attacks in force when you have only two Battlecruisers, you're in trouble. The moral is: don't overdo it with just one type of unit.

SCIENCE VESSEL
Armor: Heavy
Hit Points: 200
Ground Attack: 0
Air Attack: 0
Gas Required: 225
Minerals Required: 100

The Science Vessel isn't really an offensive weapon, but once you research all its considerable abilities it will add a great deal to your offensive and defensive powers. The Science Vessel carries a very high Vespene cost, and so usually you won't build it in quantity. However, one or two Science Vessels can turn the tide with any of its three special abilities.

The Science Vessel's Defensive Matrix special ability can set this special shield around any unit (except itself), for a much higher level of protection than normal armor and shielding. When you must get units behind enemy lines, enhance a Dropship with the Defensive Matrix so it can drop cargo without getting smoked by anti-air defenses. Give the Defensive Matrix to a Battlecruiser or Siege Tank to protect the forward unit of an assault. Uses for this shielding are limited only by your imagination. All good things must end, however, and after a short time, so does the Defensive Matrix. Keeping several Science Vessels around to protect a unit continually is a common strategy, but a protected unit still takes hits—just very small ones.

Fig. 2-21. A unit with a Defensive Matrix isn't invulnerable, but it's darned close.

The Electromagnetic Pulse Shockwave special ability is effective only against units that use special electronics or have shielding. The EMP Shockwave removes special energy or shielding from units within its blast radius (including your own). Obviously, this has no practical application against the entirely biological Zerg, but what better way to eliminate Protoss units' shielding?

One popular way to use the EMP Shockwave is to punch a hole in enemy lines by reducing the shields of all units in a given area, evening the playing field for an assault.

Fig. 2-22. Irradiate is extremely useful against tightly grouped biological units. Otherwise, it can be a waste of energy.

The Science Vessels' third special ability is Irradiate. This wide-area weapon does considerable damage to all biological units, and can wipe out a cluster quickly. Try not to use Irradiate unless you have a terrific opportunity—say, if eight Hydralisks are clumped together just asking for it. Using Irradiate on lone units usually is an inefficient use of Science Vessel energy, so choose your targets carefully. An exception to this would be using Irradiate to take out a lone Overlord that is spotting for a group of units, and then bringing in cloaked Wraiths.

DROPSHIP

Armor: Heavy
Hit Points: 150
Ground Attack: 0
Air Attack: 0
Attack Range: 0
Gas Required: 100
Minerals Required: 100

The Dropship is the Terrans' air transport unit. It has medium speed and no attack or defense values, and it isn't particularly well-protected with hit points. Anytime you use a Dropship, you must back it up with other units. Enemy air units can destroy an exposed Dropship quickly. Having even a Science Vessel as a distraction can make all the difference.

Often the best way to avoid getting your Dropships pummeled by enemy defenses is to destroy those defenses before your Dropship even arrives. In Mission 1, "First Strike," for example, it's best to use your Dropships to unload units on the ridges above the enemy defenses and let your units clear out the Spore Colonies first. Once a path is cleared, your Dropships can fly in with relative ease. The bottom line—if you're carrying mission-sensitive cargo, don't risk flying a Dropship into hostile territory unless it's well-protected by Wraiths.

Fig. 2-23. Dropships are vulnerable, so protect them well.

Terran Structures

Terran structures share a characteristic that sets them apart from those of other species—mobility. Nearly all Terran structures can lift themselves off the ground and hover to a new location, albeit very slowly. This enables you to move a Barracks or a Starport from one side of the map to the other when you lack the resources to build. Don't undervalue this ability.

Terran structures are unique in that they will deteriorate to the point of destruction if they are damaged badly enough. When a Terran structure's health bar turns red, it will continue to deteriorate (one click at a time) until the building eventually blows up. This applies to all Terran structures, and can be a good way to move more quickly through enemy Terran bases because once a structure is damaged badly, you can be sure it'll blow up shortly. The one caveat to this is that an SCV can repair a damaged structure and bring it back out of the red zone, thus halting the deterioration process.

In strategic terms, the most important structures you'll build are Missile Turrets and Bunkers, because of their implicit defensive qualities.

Bunkers

You can use Bunkers stocked with Marines for both air and ground defense, and even as an offensive weapon of sorts. It's possible to "leapfrog" your Bunkers, building them closer and closer to enemy territory; this establishes a defensive bulkhead again and again as you press forward.

TURRETS

Turrets, on the other hand, are exclusively defensive, and not only for their ability to fire on air units. Turrets are detector units, and can spot cloaked enemies as they approach. This skill can be the Turret's most valuable asset: without the detecting Turret, a base under attack by an invisible enemy soon becomes rubble.

Placing Turrets around a base is always a safe bet. It will defend against both air attacks and cloaked invaders.

The Zerg Force

When you fight as the Zerg, things change quite a bit. First, the Zerg rely heavily on mass quantities of cheap units, rather than a few superpowerful weapons. This means you must change your strategic attitudes to succeed.

All Zerg units are biological. As such, all heal themselves over time. A unit or structure just one point from destruction can recover, given time enough.

The Zerg have a different way of building units. Rather than training or manufacturing a unit, they mutate Larvae (always squirming around the Hatchery, Lair, and Hive) into the units they need. Although Drones harvest minerals and Vespene Gas, they also can mutate into structures. To "build" a structure, you must have a Drone to spare, because it becomes the structure and is lost forever.

Zerg Overlords are the equivalent of Terran Supply Depots and the Protoss Pylons. In order to continue to build Zerg units, you must have a sufficient number of Overlords to allow units to be built. Simply put, Overlords are the Zerg's supply lines. Each Overlord can be responsible for as many as seven units. When all your Overlords are occupied, you must build more.

They may not be as technologically advanced as the Terrans or Protoss, but the Zerg are a powerful force in their own right.

Ground Units

The Zerg are renowned for their overwhelming numbers. Vast swarms of Zerglings will rip the flesh off enemy units with a zeal unknown to other species. The Zerg are bred to fight, and their ground units epitomize the ferocity programmed into them over years of genetic alteration. Using a balance of Zerg forces increases your chance for success in any battle.

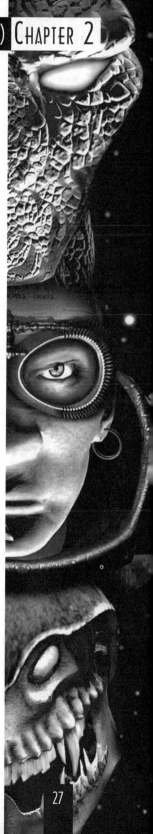

ZERGLING

Armor: Light
Hit Points: 35
Ground Attack: 5
Air Attack: 0
Attack Range: 0*
Gas Required: 0
Minerals Required: 50

The Zergling is the base unit of the Zerg ground forces. A vicious little creature, it can shred a defenseless enemy in seconds. Plus, it's cheap to produce: 50 minerals gets you two Zerglings! This makes them ideal for quick defense if an undefended base comes under attack. Just get your Hatchery to build three Eggs' worth of Zerglings, and soon you'll have six Zerglings hopping around just dying to attack the enemy.

Fig. 2-24. Zerglings can provide a quick fix when your base is caught in a tight situation.

The Zerglings' supply cost also is low, accruing only half a supply point each. This makes it the perfect unit to create in bulk. It doesn't take long to create two dozen Zerglings to use in quick, swarming attacks. Zerglings are fast, and when upgraded fully, can cover a lot of ground rapidly.

Zerglings are particularly effective when used with a group of Hydralisks. They'll move in and attack directly, distracting the enemy, while the Hydralisks pound the opposition from afar.

* Must be hand-to-hand combat.

Fig. 2-25. Siege Tanks can make dead Zerglings in a hurry.

The Zergling has its limitations, of course. It's particularly vulnerable to attacks from Siege Tanks, Firebats, Carriers, and even Radiation: anything that casts a wave of destruction over a wide area isn't good for Zerglings. A group of Zerglings in range of a Siege Tank will be turned to dust before they can turn and run, so keep aware of their limitations.

The Zergling, more than any other unit, can surprise, bewilder, and overwhelm an opponent.

BROODLING

Armor: Light
Hit Points: 30
Ground Attack: 4*
Air Attack: 0
Attack Range: 0**

Broodlings aren't mutated, but spawned from Queens that have learned Spawn Broodling behavior. They also require energy.

Broodlings cause massive damage when they first hit the enemy, and then attack much like Zerglings. A Broodling's life cycle is only as long as its energy bar. When the energy runs out, so does the Broodling.

NOTE

The Spawn Broodling ability works this way: The Zerg Queen targets an enemy ground unit (nonrobotic) and uses Spawn Broodling. The target unit is destroyed and two Broodlings come into play for the Zerg.

* Attack value limited against some units (see Appendix A).

** Must be hand-to-hand combat.

Fig. 2-26. Once you've researched to the point where you can use Broodlings, they can come in very handy.

Broodlings are a great way to get units to places easily accessible from the air. Whether your forces on the front lines need support or you just want to pop a few units into an enemy base to cause some chaos, the Broodling provides an easy solution. Five or six Queens can generate a substantial mobile attack force for striking deep into enemy territory.

HYDRALISK

Armor: Medium
Hit Points: 80
Ground Attack: 10*
Air Attack: 10*
Attack Range: 5
Gas Required: 25
Minerals Required: 75

The Hydralisk is a core unit of any Zerg attack force, acting somewhat like a bigger, stronger Marine. Their attacks pack a wallop both on land and in the air, making them versatile units that can both attack and defend a position against nearly any enemy.

* Attack value limited against some units (see Appendix A).

Fig. 2-27. When you can keep Hydralisks in groups, they're very effective against air units.

The Hydralisk's ranged attack allows you to use it like a mobile Spore Colony that can protect other units from air attack or defend your base the same way. The Hydralisk is most effective in groups of eight or more, making it difficult for enemy units to eliminate any one Hydralisk before the group can take them out.

Fig. 2-28. Because they're so versatile, always keep a few Hydralisks at your base.

A popular attack coordinates a group of Hydralisks and another group or two of Zerglings. The Zerglings occupy enemy forces while the slower Hydralisks move into position and start their ranged attacks. This is a classic,

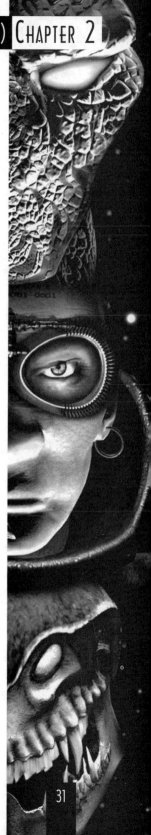

but another effective tactic uses Hydralisks as backup for Guardians. Essentially bombers, Guardians can do major damage to ground targets, but they're incapable of firing back when attacked by air. This is where Hydralisks come in. A group of 12 Hydralisks and 12 Guardians can move over a map together and crush enemy bases very effectively. Use the Hydralisks to blow enemy aircraft out of the sky while the Guardians concentrate on enemy ground units.

Lurker

Armor: Light
Hit Points: 125
Ground Attack: 20
Air Attack: 0
Attack Range: 6
Gas Required: 100
Minerals Required: 50

The Lurker is a new unit for *Brood War*, and it has one of the coolest attacks ever. The Lurker burrows (even if you haven't researched burrowing) and lies in wait for enemy units to happen by. When one gets near, the Lurker sends a line of spikes through the ground to heavily damage the enemy. A pair of Lurkers can take out a group of Marines fairly quickly, if the Marines are dumb enough to hang around.

The Lurker's only drawback is that it has no attack or defense when it isn't burrowed. And even when it's burrowed, it can be spotted by enemy detector units or Sensor Sweeps. These drawbacks aside, the Lurker is an excellent addition to the Zerg force, providing extra elements of surprise and defense.

Fig. 2-29. The Lurker will protect your base against ground attacks, and it's also good for blocking narrow valleys or peninsulas.

DRONE

Armor: Light
Hit Points: 40
Ground Attack: 5
Air Attack: 0
Attack Range: 5
Gas Required: 0
Minerals Required: 50

The Drone, like the SCV, isn't designed for attack purposes. In a pinch, though, it has an attack capability slightly greater than that of its Terran counterpart. Just remember that once a Drone mutates into a structure it's lost forever. Its biological essence creates the new structure, and is no longer available for other uses. Therefore, you must create an extra Drone for every structure you build. If you forget this, you'll end up with lots of structures and no Drones to harvest minerals and Vespene.

Fig. 2-30. It takes the life of one Drone to create each structure you need.

ULTRALISK

Armor: Heavy
Hit Points: 400
Ground Attack: 20
Air Attack: 0
Attack Range: 1
Gas Required: 200
Minerals Required: 200

The Ultralisk may be a biological unit, but you can consider it a powerful tank. With its 400 hit points, the Ultralisk is a powerhouse that can take down medium-sized enemy units easily. It may be slow, but it still should be a part of every balanced strike force. The Ultralisk is fairly slow if it's not upgraded, but it's an awesome fighting machine if you put out the resources to upgrade it's speed via Anabolic Synthesis and its armor via Chitnous Plating. This upgrade can be researched in the Ultralisk Cavern.

Fig. 2-31. Four or five Ultralisks can level an enemy base rapidly.

Its one limitation is its size: if many small units (such as Zerglings) attack it at once, it will take far more hits than it has as it destroys the enemy one by one. Therefore, it's often a good idea to keep some support units nearby to back up the Ultralisk if it gets into trouble. Protect your Ultralisks from these kinds of attacks and they can last you an entire scenario.

Fig. 2-32. A swarm of Zerglings can shred a lone Ultralisk, so always keep support units nearby.

Some players use their Ultralisks for mop-up after flushing the main enemy force from its base. Other units do most of the fighting while the Ultralisks hang back and wait for calm. When the situation stabilizes (that is, when all enemy units are dead), the Ultralisks can come in and make short work of the enemy infrastructure.

DEFILER

Armor: Medium
Hit Points: 80
Ground Attack: 0
Air Attack: 0
Gas Required: 150
Minerals Required: 25

The Defiler is a relatively high-level Zerg creature. It requires plenty of research to bring it up to attack standards, but once it's up to snuff it can provide some helpful abilities.

As can many Zerg units, the Defiler can burrow. There are two excellent reasons to do so:

▼ to regain lost health or energy after an attack
▼ to lie in wait for unsuspecting enemy units to wander by

In either case, burrowing requires that you monitor your units frequently, keeping an eye out for an opportune time to pop back to the surface.

Fig. 2-33. The Dark Swarm can provide excellent cover from airborne enemy units.

35

The Dark Swarm ability does have practical applications. It's basically a form of air cover for your units. Launching a Dark Swarm over a group of threatened ground units can protect them from airborne peril.

Plague works somewhat like the Terran Science Vessel's Irradiate ability. It can cover a fairly large area with putrid gases and damaging spores. An effective way to use Plague is to send a couple of Zerglings toward an enemy base; when a group of enemies emerges to fight, launch Plague at them. It may not kill them, but biological units will sustain significant damage.

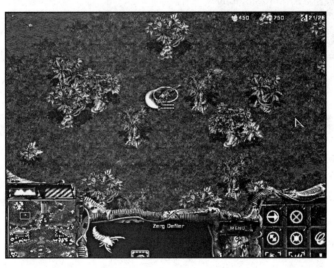

Fig. 2-34. The Defiler can restore its energy by eating another of your Zerg creatures. Yuck.

The Defiler's Consume command allows it to eat its fellow Zerg to boost its energy for a Dark Swarm or Plague. It may be a good idea to group a few Zerglings with the Defilers so they'll have something to consume when their energy gets low.

INFESTED TERRAN
Armor: Light
Hit Points: 60
Ground Attack: 500
Air Attack: 0
Attack Range: 1
Gas Required: 50
Minerals Required: 100

You may not get many chances to use the Infested Terran in *Starcraft*, but it's still an important unit. After you infest a Terran Command Center, you can produce these zombie-like kamikaze soldiers. When they near an enemy, they explode into a powerful cloud of toxic gases; the concussion devastates nearby units.

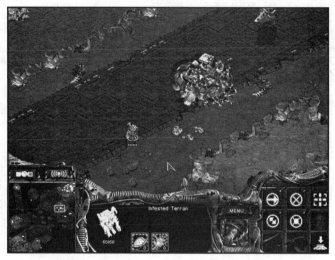

Fig. 2-35. An Infested Terran is an impressive weapon, but it's hard to get.

To infest a Command Center, you first must damage it into the red zone. Then hurry to get a Queen to infest it before it explodes (remember, Terran units pushed into the red zone deteriorate until they explode).

SPORE COLONY

Armor: Heavy
Hit Points: 400
Ground Attack: 0
Air Attack: 15
Attack Range: 7
Gas Required: 0
Minerals Required: 50

The Spore Colony attacks passing air units and, as a detector unit, spots cloaked vessels or units of any kind. The Spore Colony is converted from a Creep Colony and continues to nourish the Creep.

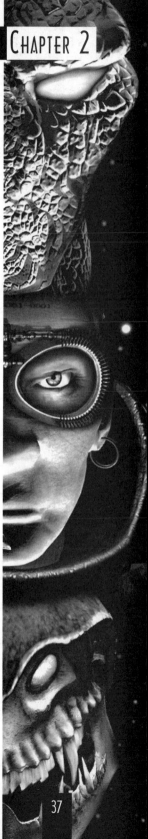

Fig. 2-36. Place Spore
Colonies in groups of three
or four for protection.

As with Missile Turrets (Terran) and Photon Cannons (Protoss), the Spore Colony is best used defensively, in groups. Several Spore Colonies can defend each other, making it less likely that a concentrated enemy attack will destroy any one colony.

SUNKEN COLONY

Armor: Heavy
Hit Points: 400
Ground Attack: 40*
Air Attack: 0
Attack Range: 7
Gas Required: 0
Minerals Required: 50

The Sunken Colony is kin to the Spore Colony and defends against ground-based attacks. The Sunken Colony, too, derives from the Creep Colony and continues to nourish the Creep even after conversion. Sunken Colonies work by thrusting a huge, tongue-like appendage under the ground toward its foe. The tendril that emerges does plenty of damage to the enemy.

* Attack value limited against some units (see Appendix A).

Fig. 2-37. Like Spore Colonies, Sunken Colonies benefit from tight groupings.

Placing Sunken Colonies close together is even more effective than grouping Spore Colonies. Any units venturing onto the Creep where there are three or four Sunken Colonies soon will be pushing up daisies. Sunken Colonies are a crucial Zerg defense, so don't skimp.

Egg

> Armor: Heavy
> Hit Points: 200
> Ground Attack: 0
> Air Attack: 0
> Attack Range: 0
> Gas Required: 0
> Minerals Required: 0

The Egg is simply a Larva mutating into a unit. Eggs are surprisingly resilient; it's unusual to see an Egg destroyed before it has a chance to hatch, although it can happen. If your Eggs are under attack, try to distract the attacker until the Egg can hatch.

Fig. 2-38. Eggs are surprisingly tough, but a persistent enemy can kill them.

Air Units

The Zerg have a variety of air units, each geared to specific tasks. This can be a great advantage, but it can be difficult to anticipate which units you'll need in a given situation. Fortunately, Zerg air units generally cost the least of any species', making it possible for you to have both a balanced ground attack and a balanced air attack!

The Zerg have a new unit, the Devourer, in their arsenal, and it packs a punch.

DEVOURER

Armor: Medium
Hit Points: 250
Ground Attack: 0
Air Attack: 25
Attack Range: 6
Gas Required: 50
Minerals Required: 150

The Devourer is one of two new Zerg units in *Starcraft: Brood War*. It has an air-only attack (it can't attack ground units) that affects nearby units as well as the target unit. Devourers, like Guardians, must be evolved from a Mutalisk.

The main attack's secondary effect is like a splash. It hits adjacent units with Acid Spores that make the affected units more vulnerable to damage and increases the time it takes for them to fire their next shot. This bonus can cripple a group of enemy air units quickly.

Fig. 2-39. The Devourer works best against groups of enemy air units.

MUTALISK
Armor: Light
Hit Points: 120
Ground Attack: 9
Air Attack: 9
Attack Range: 3
Gas Required: 100
Minerals Required: 100

The Mutalisk is the Zerg basic air unit. It has nicely balanced air and ground attacks and it's relatively cheap. It's possible to play a complete mission using no other air units (other than Overlords, of course).

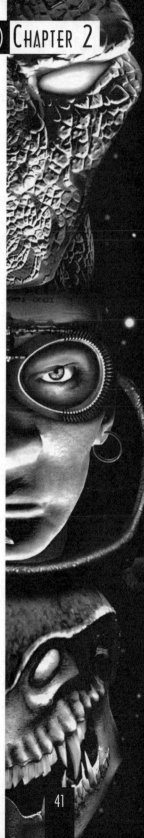

Fig. 2-40. "Just say no" to your own death. Use Mutalisks in groups of three or more.

The Mutalisk's Glave Wurm attack hits its target and then continues to another nearby unit or structure. This cumulative attack can be devastating when a large group of Mutalisks attacks a bunch of Marines. Each Mutalisk shot breaks away, hits a Marine, breaks away again, hits another Marine, and so on. The damage factor decreases by half every time the Wurm splits, but even so, the multiple attack values of many Mutalisks add up quickly.

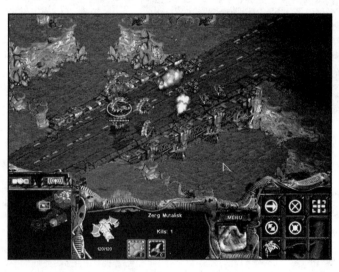

Fig. 2-41. The cumulative effects of the Mutalisk's multiple attacks can wreak havoc on a group of Marines.

The downside is the Mutalisk's poor range (3), which forces it to get very close to its target. This means Marines (with a range of 4) have an easy time against Mutalisks. In force, however, they're very effective in most situations.

GUARDIAN

Armor: Heavy
Hit Points: 150
Ground Attack: 20
Air Attack: 0
Attack Range: 8
Gas Required: 100
Minerals Required: 50

Guardians are actually Mutalisks that have metamorphosed after having entered a cocoon state. You must earn the ability to create Guardians, and this usually won't happen until your base is fairly well-established. The Guardian acts as a "bomber," hurling explosive gobs of acid at ground targets. Its awesome attack power (20) packs enough wallop to take out a **Missile Turret** in 10 hits (or one hit each from a group of 10 Guardians).

Fig. 2-42. The Guardian must metamorphose from a Mutalisk.

Guardians work best in groups of 10 or more. A single volley from such a group can destroy any enemy unit that has 200 or fewer hit points. Of course, 12 Guardians bombing an enemy base won't bomb it for long if the enemy attacks with air units: the Guardian is air-to-ground only. It's important to have Mutalisks standing by to defend your Guardians.

Fig. 2-43. In groups, the Guardians are bombers from hell, but they're vulnerable to air attacks.

Expense is another limiting factor. Creating a Guardian costs 100 gas and 50 minerals, plus you must metamorphose it from a Mutalisk, with a price tag of 100 gas and 150 minerals. Thus, the true cost of creating a Guardian is 200 gas and 200 minerals (ouch). Protecting that investment is very important.

QUEEN
Armor: Medium
Hit Points: 120
Ground Attack: 0
Air Attack: 0
Attack Range: 0
Gas Required: 150
Minerals Required: 100

The Queen is a unique unit. Although it can't attack enemy units directly, it can use its special abilities to great effect. The Queen isn't particularly expensive, so you can create a small pack for backup, defense, fire fighting, or as first-strike units.

The first, and perhaps handiest, of the Queen's special abilities is the Parasite. This tiny organism infects an enemy unit and allows you (the player) to see through its eyes. It can be prudent to take a Queen and move about the map (carefully) depositing Parasites on any unit it encounters. Airborne units, such as Dropships or patrolling Scouts, are ideal to infect with Parasites. These units move around the map constantly, providing an excellent view of what's going on behind enemy lines.

Fig. 2-44. Ensnare's green goo tells you the ability is working.

The Ensnare ability is a terrific asset. Ensnare slimes enemy units in green goo, slowing them down and making it easier for your forces to take them out. Use Ensnare offensively to bog down enemy units while your own file past.

Spawning Broodlings is a spectacular way to use your Queens. Spawn Broodlings shoot spores into the enemy which then hatch into Broodlings that feed on the host. This happens very quickly; in the end the host explodes, leaving behind a pair of Broodlings ready to do your bidding.

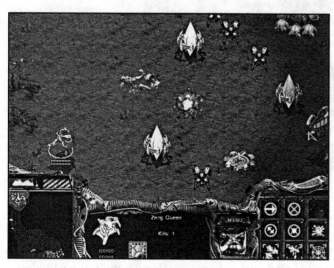

Fig. 2-45. Your Queen's Spawn Broodlings ability quickly puts vicious little critters behind enemy lines.

45

Use Infestation to capture a badly damaged Terran Command Center and get Infested Terrans. To infest a Command Center, you must get a Queen close to one that's in the red zone (nearly destroyed), and then launch Infestation at it. The Command Center will fall under Zerg control, allowing you to create Infested Terrans.

Scourge

Armor: Light

Hit Points: 25

Ground Attack: 0

Air Attack: 110

Attack Range: 1

Gas Required: 75

Minerals Required: 25

Scourges are the Zerglings of the air. They hatch two at a time from each Egg and cost only slightly more than Zerglings, making it relatively easy to create large groups of them. It's a good idea to keep a group of 12 Scourges around to defend against capital ship attacks.

Fig. 2-46. The Scourge are infamous Carrier killers.

The Scourge is essentially a kamikaze, slamming into the hull of a larger ship and exploding on contact. It really shines against Protoss Carriers; in fact, many *Starcraft* players call them "Carrier killers." A group of 12 Scourges flung at a Carrier almost certainly will destroy it, making these units quite valuable.

On the downside, they fight less well against smaller ships, and can't attack ground units.

OVERLORD

Armor: Heavy

Hit Points: 200

Ground Attack: 0

Air Attack: 0

Attack Range: 0

Gas Required: 0

Minerals Required: 100

The Overlord serves three purposes for the Zerg. First, it's the equivalent of Terran Supply Depots or Protoss Pylons; how many you need depends on how large your Zerg force is. Second, it's the Zerg Shuttle. To transport units by air, you must research Transport for your Overlords (do this in a Lair). Third, the Overlord is a detection unit that can sight cloaked enemies!

Transporting units with an Overlord is risky, but if you take the proper precautions, it needn't be stress-inducing. Protect your Overlords with Mutalisks and Scourge. Don't move your Overlords into areas with lots of anti-air resistance. Finally, upgrade Overlord Sight and Speed in the Lair/Hive. Speed is especially important, because the upgrade doubles the lumbering Overlord's rate of movement.

Fig. 2-47. Overlords are easy targets for Photon Cannons and Missile Turrets, so don't take them into hostile territory unless you have a very good reason.

Zerg Structures

Zerg structures are living organisms and can heal themselves after they take a beating. This has a substantial impact on how you manage your resources. For example, a nearly destroyed structure normally might be replaced, but in the case of the Zerg, the structure slowly will regain its hit points over time.

This makes protecting damaged structures more important than for other species, and affects the scenario in terms of both Zerg and enemy strategy. The enemy might launch a last-ditch second effort to finish off a badly damaged building rather than see its failed attack go to waste as the structure repairs itself. For the Zerg, an offensive push might be in order after fending off an attack, if only to clear the enemy out of your base so the structures have time to heal. Of course, this depends largely on your opponent's playing style, but the principles hold true.

Sunken and Spore Colonies

Sunken Colonies and Spore Colonies both derive from the Creep Colony and both continue to feed the Creep even after conversion. These two units will be largely responsible for defending your main Creep, so build them in quantity whenever you can, positioning Spore Colonies throughout the base as an air deterrent and distributing Sunken Colonies only where ground-based attacks are possible.

The Protoss Force

As you might expect, the Protoss differ in several ways from both Terrans and Zerg. They're the most technologically advanced species, but pay the greatest base cost per unit. Although in the original *Starcraft* you played the Protoss missions last, this time you'll be playing them first. If you haven't played *Starcraft* before, or even if you're already familiar with them, there are a few things you should know before you venture forth.

Protoss units enter each scenario through a Probe-opened Warp Rift. The cool thing about Probes is they need only begin the process of opening the rift; they needn't wait for the structure to appear. This way a single Probe can move around opening Warp Rifts while your other Probes happily harvest minerals and gas.

Playing as the Zerg can leave you with a throwaway attitude toward your units. Protoss units are considerably more expensive, however, so never treat them as if they're easy to replace. Novice Protoss players have lost many a game by running out of resources as they tried to create overwhelming numbers. The key to Protoss victory lies in their superior technology rather than brute force potential.

All Protoss have shields that absorb punishment before a unit takes any hits. Actual damage can't be repaired, but the shields always regenerate. This means even a Protoss unit with one hit point left can be a threat if its shields have regenerated. A Terran EMP blast can defeat your shields in one fell swoop, but unless the enemy can hit you with one of these attacks, your shields must be destroyed the old-fashioned way, one hit at a time.

Ground Units

Get ready to explore *Starcraft: Brood War*'s "high-tech" lineup of ground units. "Strong," "powerful," "fast," and "expensive" all describe the Protoss ground arsenal, but in the end it's a well-balanced set of units that stacks up fairly evenly against the other species'.

ZEALOT
Armor: Light
Shield: 80
Hit Points: 80
Ground Attack: 16
Air Attack: 0
Attack Range: 1
Gas Required: 0
Minerals Required: 100

Like the Terran Marine and Zerg Zergling, the Zealot is the basic Protoss ground unit. When it comes to attack ability, however, the Zealot is in a different league from its opposing counterparts. The Zealot has almost three times the Marine's attack power and four times the Zergling's. But nothing in life is free, and the Zealot is the most expensive base unit by 100 percent. You pay for what you get.

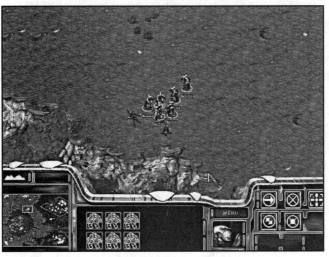

Fig. 2-48. The Zealot packs an attack of 16 and is tough enough to stand up to almost any ground attack. The downside? Zealots get pummeled from the skies.

The Zealot's weapon is the Psionic Blade; it has two (one on each arm). Thus, the Zealot has no ranged attack and must be very close to the enemy to do damage—and it can't attack air units. Therefore, it's always a good idea to take along Dragoons, Scouts, or the Templars (with Psionic Storm) to defend against air attacks whenever your Zealots are on the move. A large group of Zealots can destroy an enemy base quickly if nothing attacks from the sky.

DRAGOON

Armor: Heavy
Shield: 80
Hit Points: 100
Ground Attack: 20*
Air Attack: 20*
Attack Range: 4
Gas Required: 50
Minerals Required: 125

The Dragoon is the number two unit of the Protoss force. It's powerful, but has a longer cool-down time between firing and is considerably more expensive to produce than the Zealot. However, the Dragoon performs both ground and air attacks, and can attack on its own or back up fellow units.

* Attack value limited against some units (see Appendix A).

Fig. 2-49. The Dragoon is excellent for performing both ground and air attacks.

Because Dragoons are fast, you may be tempted to make a strike force of 10 or so to take it to the enemy—but don't. The Dragoon is an excellent unit, but 30 Zerglings will be more than 12 Dragoons can handle in the absence of backup units. A popular tactic is to move groups of Zealots and Dragoons together in much the same way as Marines and Firebats.

Fig. 2-50. Taking eight high-priced Dragoons into a pile of 30 Zerglings will give you a lesson in humility.

51

It's also a good idea to keep a small group of Dragoons around your base to back up your Photon Cannon defenses. Keeping units at home is always a good idea, but Dragoons are so fast you can move them to a hot spot without losing much time. They're effective mobile units when you need a little help quickly.

REAVER

Armor: Heavy

Shield: 80

Hit Points: 100

Ground Attack (Scarab Drone): 100*

Air Attack: 0

Attack Range: 8

Gas Required: 100

Minerals Required: 200

The Reaver is a strange unit, often called the "Ground Carrier" because of the Scarab Drones it unleashes on the enemy. Although it looks intimidating, it doesn't have weapons of its own. Instead, it builds Scarab Drones in its internal manufacturing plant and unleashes *them* on the enemy.

Fig. 2-51. The Reaver is slow, expensive, and lacks a main weapon, but it still rocks.

The Reaver can store as many as 10 Scarabs within itself and use them as necessary. When released, the Scarabs zip toward their targets and explode, causing substantial damage to nearby enemy units. Sending Scarabs into

* Attack value limited against some units (see Appendix A).

packs of enemies can give you some very satisfying results. Scarabs are also very useful for taking out structures, such as Photon Cannons and Bunkers, from afar.

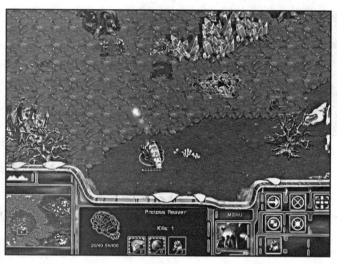

Fig. 2-52. Use care when deploying your Scarabs, or you'll end up taking out your own forces.

Reavers are effective against defensive emplacements such as Bunkers or Spore Colonies. But they're fairly easy to kill, so protect them well; if it looks like you may lose a Reaver, use up its remaining Scarabs!

HIGH TEMPLAR

Armor: Light
Shield: 40
Hit Points: 40
Ground Attack: 0
Air Attack: 0
Gas Required: 150
Minerals Required: 50

Although High Templars can fight, you should keep them back from the front lines and exploit their psychic abilities. These units are Protoss army veterans who have mastered the Psi energy running through their bodies.

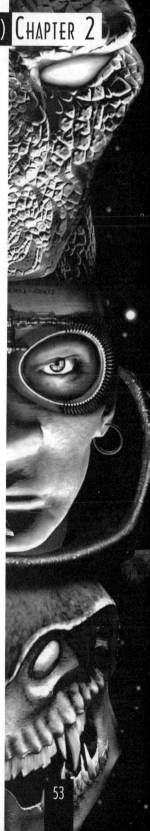

Fig. 2-53. The High Templars aren't designed for hand-to-hand combat. Stick to using their Psionic abilities and you'll be OK.

The Psionic Storm is High Templars' most powerful psionic ability. It can take out enemy units if they're grouped close together without much room to run. Because the Zerg tend to move and attack en masse, the Psionic Storm can kill off large numbers of them. Try sending a single Zealot onto a Zerg Creep. When the Hydralisks and Zerglings pop out to fight, hit them with a Psionic Storm and watch them turn to pools of blood.

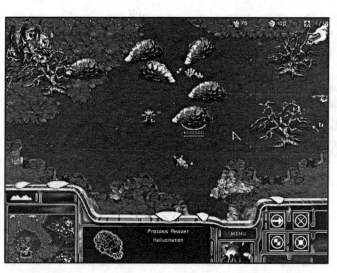

Fig. 2-54. Hallucination can fool the enemy into thinking you have more units than you really do.

Hallucination is valuable when your forces are outnumbered. It produces two illusory copies of each unit you use it on. You can see which units are real and which aren't, but the enemy can't, and often will attack the hallucinations.

The Summon Archon ability forever merges two Templars into an Archon, a powerful super-unit that's devastating to both ground and air forces.

DARK TEMPLAR

Armor: Light

Shield: 40

Hit Points: 80

Ground Attack: 40

Air Attack: 0

Attack Range: 1

Gas Required: 100

Minerals Required: 125

The Dark Templar appeared in several original *Starcraft* missions, but you never could build one for yourself. That changes in *Brood War*; not only can you build them, but they're building blocks for another new unit, the Dark Archon.

Dark Templars are excellent overall ground units. They have a powerful attack and a reasonable reservoir of hit points—and they're permanently cloaked. The latter makes it very difficult for the enemy to attack them in the absence of a nearby detector unit. Dark Templars are great for sneaking into enemy bases and wreaking havoc. There are a few missions in *Brood War* where the Dark Templars' stealth will serve you well. The Summon Dart Archon ability forever merges two Dark Templars into a Dark Archon, a powerful super-unit that has many devastating special abilities.

Fig. 2-55. Dark Templars are permanently cloaked, making them excellent stealth weapons.

ARCHON

Armor: Heavy
Shield: 350
Hit Points: 10
Ground Attack: 30
Air Attack: 30
Attack Range: 3
Gas Required: 300
Minerals Required: 100

Archons result from the union of two High Templars, and so are fairly expensive. Still, their attacks and defensive shields are so powerful, they're usually worth the expense. The Archon also is special because it can attack units both in the air and on the ground. A group of seven or eight Archons is tough for any species to stop, especially if they have backup.

Fig. 2-56. With 350 shield points, the Archon is a devastating unit.

Use the Archon as what it really is—a Heavy Assault Warrior. Building up a devastating Archon strike force can be counterproductive. If it fails, you'll have lost massive amounts of resources. Instead, use Archons to complement groupings of Dragoons and Zealots. Your Archon can inflict huge amounts of pain on any powerful enemy before it can kill your more vulnerable units.

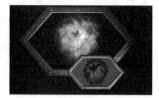

DARK ARCHON

Armor: Light

Shield: 200

Hit Points: 25

Ground Attack: 0

Air Attack: 0

Attack Range: 0

Gas Required: 200

Minerals Required: 250

The Dark Archon is arguably the game's most influential unit. Although it's of no value in melee combat, its two main abilities make it invaluable.

The Dark Archon's Mind Control ability allows you to make an enemy unit your own. Obviously, this is very powerful, so using it comes at a high cost, draining your Dark Archon's energy *and shields!* But if you can mind-control a filled enemy transport, you gain *all* the units it carries, as well as the transport itself. Of course, using Mind Control on Carriers and Battlecruisers also can be a big help to your efforts. Keeping five or six Dark Archons handy at the front lines can help you fend off—and even eliminate—enemy attacks.

The Dark Archon's Maelstrom ability affects biological units and acts like Lockdown, freezing those units in place so you can target them easily. Maelstrom's area of effect will lock down all an area's biological units so you can launch a Psionic Storm.

Fig. 2-57. Mind Control is just too cool! Watch out—being able to take over enemy units is addictive.

57

The Dark Archon also has an ability known as Feedback. When cast on a unit, Feedback will cause that unit to lose all of its mana, and also take an amount of damage equal to the mana lost. This is essentially the Dark Archon's only attack, even if it does require mana to accomplish it.

PHOTON CANNON

Armor: Heavy

Shield: 100

Hit Points: 100

Ground Attack: 20

Air Attack: 20

Attack Range: 7

Gas Required: 0

Minerals Required: 150

The Photon Cannon is perhaps the game's best defensive structure. Its cost is reasonable and it can defend against land and air targets as far as seven clicks distant. A webbing of four to six Photon Cannons near a contentious point can make the difference between victory and defeat.

Fig. 2-58. A grid of Photon Cannons can be all the defense you'll ever need.

The downside is that the Photon Cannon is relatively easy to destroy. Once you've set up a Defensive Matrix, keep a Probe handy in case you need to open a Warp Rift and bring in replacements.

PROBE

Armor: Light
Shield: 20
Hit Points: 20
Ground Attack: 5
Air Attack: 0
Attack Range: 1
Gas Required: 0
Minerals Required: 50

At 20 hit points, the Protoss Probe has the lowest HP total of any enemy counterpart, but its ability to open Warp Rifts and walk away makes up for this. Like the Terran SCV and Zerg Drone, the Probe can fight the enemy, but with so little defense (and with such a feeble attack), it's wiser to rely on Photon Cannons around your base.

Fig. 2-59. The Probe is a great base-building unit, so avoid using it for fighting.

    When setting up a base, use all your Probes to gather resources except one: it can open all the Warp Rifts you need without interrupting the flow of resources.

Air Units

As with the other Protoss units, Protoss air units tend to be expensive, but, again, they're also very powerful. Amass a large enough resource base, and you can build the air units you need to win. Many players believe *Starcraft* (and *Brood War*) is won or lost in the skies. That's open to interpretation, but never doubt the importance of having a solid air force. The new Protoss air unit, the Corsair, has an impact you can feel from the first mission you have access to it.

Scout

Armor: Heavy
Shield: 100
Hit Points: 150
Ground Attack: 8
Air Attack: 28*
Attack Range: 4
Gas Required: 100
Minerals Required: 300

Building Scout "victory fleets" to fly around kicking butt is a popular pastime, but it's probably not the wisest course of action. Creating such a group requires crushing amounts of mineral resources.

The Scout may sound like it's, well, a scout, but it's really more like a full-featured fighter than a reconnaissance ship. The Scout can attack both air and ground targets, but it's best suited to air-to-air combat.

Fig. 2-60. Use the Scout in small groups to flank enemy forces.

* Attack value limited against some units (see Appendix A).

Scouts are an excellent way to flank the enemy, ideally in groups of three to five. If you attack an enemy force from the front, sending two groups of three Scouts each against enemy flanks to generate a chaotic enemy overcorrection can yield you the battle.

Fig. 2-61. A Scout (or two) around your base is worth three in the bush.

Its great speed makes the Scout the perfect Protoss firefighter, flying from hot spot to hot spot to keep the peace when the enemy gets cocky. This includes attacks against your own base, so keep at least one Scout at home to be on the safe side.

CORSAIR
Armor: Heavy
Shield: 80
Hit Points: 100
Ground Attack: 0
Air Attack: 5*
Attack Range: 5
Gas Required: 100
Minerals Required: 150

The Corsair is new to *Brood War*, but its Disruption Web is a critical component in many missions. Although the Corsair can fight only in air-to-air combat, and its attack is very weak, it has a penchant for getting into fights. If an enemy air

* Attack value limited against some units (see Appendix A).

unit comes anywhere near, the Corsair will sprint off after it, even if its path is over 100 Spore Colonies. Needless to say, you'll be using the Hold command a lot when you work with Corsairs.

The Disruption Web special ability generates a white web that prevents anything under it from attacking you—while *you* attack from the air! Thus, it's good to group Corsairs with Scouts so the Scouts can perform air-to-ground attacks while the Corsairs launch Disruption Webs.

Fig. 2-62. The Disruption Web will be your best friend in several missions.

CARRIER

Armor: Heavy
Shield: 150
Hit Points: 300
Ground Attack (Interceptors): 6
Air Attack (Interceptors): 6
Attack Range: 8
Gas Required: 250
Minerals Required: 350
Interceptor Hit Points: 40
Interceptor Shield: 40

The Carrier is perhaps *Starcraft*'s most powerful weapon. The Carrier itself has no innate attack ability. After you upgrade it, however, it can carry up to eight Interceptors that can each attack air and ground units with a value of 5. In other words, a pair of Carriers can unleash a hornet's nest of Interceptors that can destroy air and ground units alike in a frenzied bloodbath.

Fig. 2-63. A fully loaded Carrier is an awesome weapon that can panic the enemy.

The Carrier can land the killing blow in an attack on enemy forces. Even if the battle is a standoff, a fully loaded Carrier or two can turn the tide in a hurry. Send a Carrier into an area of enemy units, click to "attack" a general location, and your Interceptors will hunt new targets continually. They'll swarm and swarm until there's nothing left to kill. Interceptors often will draw the attention (and fire) of enemy units and structures, but they're so fast they rarely take a hit.

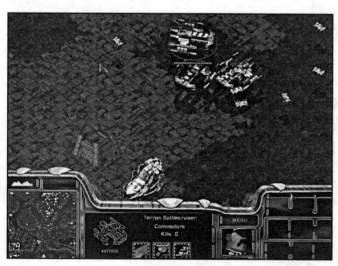

Fig. 2-64. A few Battlecruisers can take out a Carrier in one shot, so don't get cocky.

63

Carriers aren't invulnerable, however. A dozen Scourge ("Carrier Killers") can bring an end to a Carrier in about 10 seconds. And a trio of Battlecruisers with the Yamato Cannon can take out a Carrier in one shot. This doesn't mean you shouldn't use Carriers; just don't rely on them too heavily.

ARBITER

Armor: Heavy
Shield: 150
Hit Points: 200
Ground Attack: 10*
Air Attack: 10*
Attack Range: 5
Gas Required: 350
Minerals Required: 100

The Arbiter performs three key functions for the Protoss. A capable warship that can attack both air and ground units, its innate abilities make this vessel an essential part of a balanced Protoss fleet.

The Arbiter emanates a Cloak that conceals any units in its radius. The Arbiter itself isn't cloaked, but it looks a lot less threatening approaching an enemy base than a fleet of four Carriers. Only detector units can see them coming.

Fig. 2-65. Arbiters can hide more ships than you might think, but its Cloak is useless around detector units.

* Attack value limited against some units (see Appendix A).

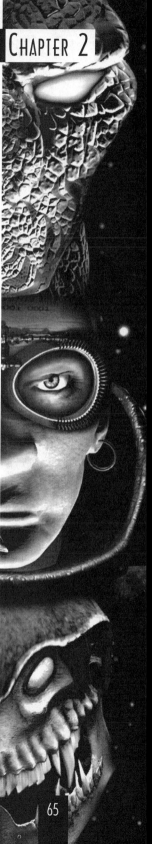

Recall, another powerful Arbiter ability, acts like a teleport for units within a certain radius. A few Arbiters near the front lines can teleport groups of units to the action instantaneously, bypassing the time-consuming and risky business of using Shuttles. There are numerous ways to use Recall, including teleporting units to an undefended base that's under attack.

Fig. 2-66. Use the Stasis Field to disable enemy units and even the playing field (or tilt it toward you).

The Stasis Field is a powerful ability that can reduce the burden of combat substantially. Use the Stasis Field to take several enemy units out of the picture until you're ready to deal with them. For example, if your forces come up against a large enemy group, you can put half the enemy group in a Stasis Field while you attack (and kill) the other half. When the Stasis Field wears off, you can kill those units.

OBSERVER

Armor: Light
Shield: 20
Hit Points: 40
Ground Attack: 0
Air Attack: 0
Attack Range: 0
Gas Required: 75
Minerals Required: 25

The Observer is a permanently cloaked scout unit that's also a detector (it can see other cloaked units). It's usually a good idea to place a few Observers over strategic points on the map (such as resource nodes) to monitor enemy troop movement. Because they're cloaked, they can be your best source of enemy intelligence, so keep one or two in action at all times.

Fig. 2-67. "Keeping up with the Joneses" is an important part of *Starcraft*, and a pair of Observers can help you see what the Joneses are up to.

SHUTTLE
Armor: Heavy
Shield: 60
Hit Points: 80
Ground Attack: 0
Air Attack: 0
Attack Range: 0
Gas Required: 0
Minerals Required: 200

The Shuttle is, well, a shuttle. For the Protoss, it's the only mechanical way to move units through the air. The Arbiter's Recall ability moves units faster, but the Shuttle is still an effective way to ferry troops across large or impassable areas.

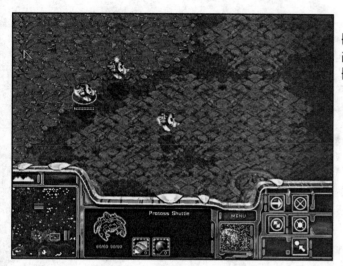

Fig. 2-68. Shuttles are important units even for the high-flying Protoss.

Protoss Structures

Protoss structures have no special ability to heal or move, but they do have shields that recharge continually. This defensive boost provides the protection they need to survive attacks from competitors.

The fact that Probes needn't sit around waiting for structures to be built helps you acquire more structures sooner than would be possible otherwise. One Probe can do the work of opening the Warp Rifts, while all the others collect resources.

PHOTON CANNONS

The Photon Cannon is the all-purpose Protoss defensive weapon structure, and it serves that function well. Able to attack both air and ground targets, a grouping of Photon Cannons can provide enough of a deterrent to halt attacks from human opponents permanently, and if the computer is bent on continuing, the Photon grid will mow the enemy down. Always keep at least three closely placed Photon Cannons at your base entrance.

General Strategies

If the original *Starcraft* was an amazing game, embodying all that an awesome strategy game should be, its sequel, *Starcraft: Brood War*, is even better, incorporating detailed cutscenes with intense action.

As with the original game, success in *Starcraft: Brood War* hinges on using solid, proven strategies. You should feel free to experiment, but ultimately you must realize that failing to follow at least a basic strategic framework can mean bitter defeat.

This chapter provides general strategies for all three species. These have the blessing of the Blizzard testing department, so you're well-advised to familiarize yourself with them.

The strategies and tips that follow apply to both single- and multiplayer games.

> **NOTE**
>
> Special thanks must go out to Blizzard employees Rob Pardo, Eric Dodds, Frank Gilson, John Lagrave, and Derek Simmons for their infinite strategic wisdom.

Terrans

This "middle-of-the-road" species offers a good balance of numbers (of units) and technology. The Terran arsenal includes several new twists, including missile upgrades for Goliaths and, of course, the two new units (Medic and Frigate).

There are probably as many Terran attack and defense strategies as there are players, but these key ideas will help you through the rough stuff.

General Strategies and Tips

▼ Hotkey the Comsat Station (yes, you can do that) to 9 and 0 to get a Sensor Sweep quickly without having to click on it. To get a sweep on demand, first press the Station's hotkey, and then Ⓢ. Getting a Sensor Sweep can be critical if your troops are under attack from cloaked units, because the sweep will reveal enemy unit locations and hidden enemy units.

▼ For defense, build Bunkers (filled with Marines) and Missile Turrets together. It's also a good idea to place Siege Tanks beside them. This combination provides an extremely tenacious defense that's difficult for the enemy to penetrate.

▼ When both Comsat Stations and Yamato Cannons become available, use them together to take advantage of the Yamato's superior range. For example, to take out a Missile Turret, sweep the Missile Turret area with a Sensor Sweep, and then target it with a Yamato strike. The Battlecruiser will move in to take its shot while still outside the Missile Turret's range.

▼ This is underhanded, but effective: Build a Factory or Barracks behind the enemy's position and start cranking out units for a backside attack. If you can't afford to build there, or can't get an SCV to that position, fly an existing structure into position, and then begin building.

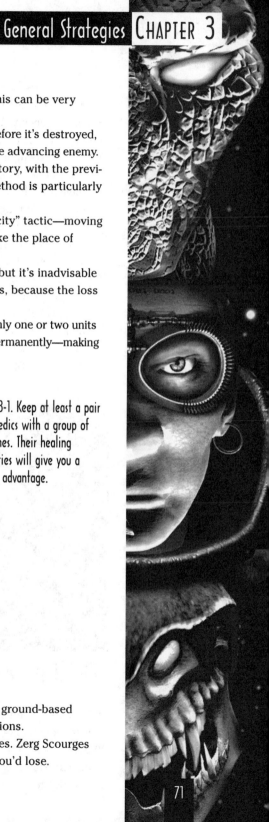

▼ Use the Science Vessel's Irradiate ability on biological units. This can be very effective, even against Templars or Defilers.

▼ To prevent enemy movement, place Bunkers at choke points. Before it's destroyed, a carefully placed Bunker can do huge amounts of damage to the advancing enemy. Build Bunkers "leapfrog" fashion, ever deeper into enemy territory, with the previous Bunker protecting the Bunker under construction. This method is particularly useful against the Zerg.

▼ Because Terran structures are mobile, you can use a "moving city" tactic—moving your city across the map as needed. Upgraded Goliaths can take the place of Missile Turrets here.

▼ Medics can have a huge impact on the outcome of a skirmish, but it's inadvisable to have more than two Medics per group of 12 Marines/Firebats, because the loss of firepower counteracts the Medics' healing ways.

Use the Medic's Optical Flare to great effect in situations where only one or two units impede your path. It shortens the enemy unit's range of sight—permanently—making it easy to destroy from a safe distance.

Fig. 3-1. Keep at least a pair of Medics with a group of Marines. Their healing abilities will give you a huge advantage.

Against the Zerg

Build lots of Firebats. The Zerg are an organic species with mostly ground-based attacks. Firebats always are cost-effective against Zerg ground minions.

Use more Battlecruisers defensively, especially in multiplayer games. Zerg Scourges can take out a Battlecruiser for half its cost. In a resource battle, you'd lose.

▼ Use Parasite-infected units to fight the enemy. Never keep them around your base, because the enemy sees everything they see.

▼ Take out enemy Guardians at all costs: they can reduce your base to rubble quickly.

▼ Keep Wraiths or Battlecruisers around for this purpose.

▼ *Never* leave an outpost Command Center for the Zerg to infest, or Infested Terrans soon will be blowing up all around you. And that isn't pretty.

When attacking a Zerg base, always take out the underlying tech-tree buildings first. It's tempting to go for the Hatcheries, but it's more crippling to your opponents to lose the structures they need to build advanced units. Take out Zerg structures in this order: Spire, Ultralisk Cavern, Hydralisk Den, Spawning Pool, and Queen's Nest.

▼ Frigate Valkyries are extremely effective against the Zerg. A pair of Valkyries will eliminate a group of Overminds quickly; they simply can't get away in time.

▼ Use the Medic's Restoration ability to remove Plague and Parasites from your units. Medics can be especially effective in saving costly units such as Battlecruisers from the Defiler's Plague, so always keep a Medic nearby when facing the Zerg.

Fig. 3-2. Use Firebats to deal with the Zergs' vast numbers.

Against the Protoss

▼ Firebats are important only against Zealots, so don't go crazy building them. Make just enough to keep Zealot groups at bay.

▼ Build Ghosts for defense. They're a little too expensive to produce in bulk for offense. However, when an enemy Carrier or Reaver comes by, you can use the Lockdown ability to neutralize them.

▼ Because it removes their shields, Science Vessels' EMP ability is especially effective against the Protoss. The EMP is as effective for attack as it is for defense.

▼ If the Protoss are employing Arbiters, use a Yamato Cannon to take them out quickly and reveal cloaked units.

▼ Use a Comsat Sensor Sweep to check for Observers in areas where you plan to use cloaked units. Cloaked Observers will locate your own cloaked units.

▼ Keep Missile Turrets around your entire base as an early warning system. If this prevents just one Shuttle from dropping a pair of Reavers, it was worth it.

▼ Upgraded Goliaths can butt heads effectively with a group of Scouts. It's always a good idea to keep some Goliaths around for air defense.

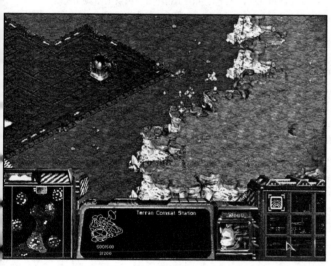

Fig. 3-3. Use your Comsat Sensor to sweep for Observers.

Zerg

The Zerg are entirely biological and lack high-end units that compare with those of the Protoss or Terrans. Therefore, they must employ different tactics to achieve the same ends. The Zerg have two new units in *Brood War*—the Devourer and the Lurker. Both can turn the tide in a close battle.

General Strategies and Tips

▼ When enemy air units enter your base, have a Defiler use a Dark Swarm over your Hydralisks. This renders them impervious to enemy air attacks and frees them to shoot the bad guys out of the sky.

▼ Build Zerglings and Hydralisks initially, but remember that Zealots and Firebats can go through Zerglings like a hot knife through butter. Use your Zerglings and Hydralisks to attack Marines and Dragoons.

▼ Guardians are your heavy attack force. A group of 12 will destroy virtually any land-based group, as long as they stay at a safe distance and are willing to retreat. On larger maps, use Nydus Canals to connect your bases. This allows you to build a much smaller defense force at each base, because you can teleport units from one base to another very quickly.

▼ Scourges are most effective against enemy capital ships, such as Carriers and Battlecruisers, so keep a bunch around for this. Scourges are significantly less effective against Scouts or Wraiths, so don't waste them against these units.

▼ Try to keep a large perimeter of Sunken Colonies and Spore Colonies around important structures in your base. This way, even if you leave your base lightly defended, the colonies can work to eliminate the enemy threat.

▼ When attacking an enemy base with a strictly Zergling force, don't waste time attacking enemy units. Instead, send your Zerglings to attack enemy structures; a group of Zerglings can bring down a structure quickly.

▼ The Zerg ability to create masses of a certain type of unit by morphing multiple Larvae can quickly shift the battle in your favor, if you choose the units well. Extra Hatcheries increase your ability to manufacture lots of new units quickly.

▼ Lurkers are an awesome defensive weapon, especially around your Hatcheries. If an attack force enters without a detector unit, a burrowed Lurker will kick enemy butt when they venture near. Place several Lurkers in and around your base, along with Spore and Sunken Colonies, for the best effect.

Fig. 3-4. Burrow a few Lurkers around your base for defense.

Against the Terrans

▼ Have your Queen use its Ensnare ability on a group of cloaked Wraiths, and then put Parasites on as many of them as you can. This eliminates their ability to cloak.

▼ To take out a Terran player quickly, build lots of Zerglings. Upgrade their speed and attack abilities, and then launch them at the enemy in groups of 12. Speed is important; you don't want the Terrans to build up a large force of Firebats.

▼ Hydralisks, the Zergs' bread-and-butter unit, can be effective in both ground and air attack and defense. A Zerg player without Hydralisks is a Zerg player who's probably losing.

▼ Use your Queen's Spawn Broodling ability on Tanks and Goliaths, and use Ensnare on cloaked Wraiths and Ghosts. If a cloaked unit is escaping, infest it with a Parasite so it can never cloak again.

▼ Use the Plague where Supply Depots are grouped closely together. After a few Plagues, the affected depots will proceed into the red and eventually will blow up (unless repaired).

▼ Try to attack a Terran Command Center early on to open the door for Infestation. You'll need a Queen for this, though, so don't risk any units until you're ready.

▼ Keep your Hydralisks and Zerglings burrowed until heavy enemy units come close; then spring the surprise. Keeping several groups of units burrowed in defensive positions is always a good idea.

▼ Devourers are high-end air-to-air units that are very effective against Terran air units. The Devourer attack's splash factor leaves Acid Spores on enemy units that render them more vulnerable to attack, and hamper their ability to attack you.

▼ Lurkers can chew up Marines and spit them out before they know what happened. Be sure to move your burrowed Lurkers after they do their thing, or responding enemy detector units will come to reveal them.

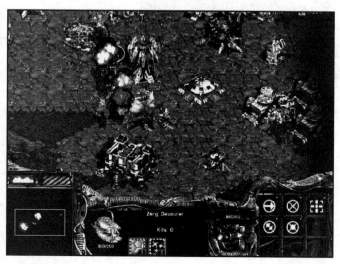

Fig. 3-5. Devourers cause splash damage to units adjacent to an attack.

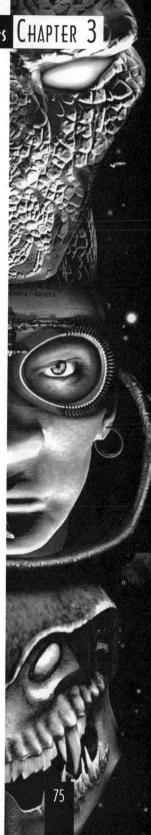

Against the Protoss

▼ In the early going, build Hydralisks and more Hydralisks. They're very effective against Zealots, Dragoons, and Scouts.

▼ Watch out for Observers. Fortunately, the Overlord is a detector unit, and you usually have plenty of Overlords to patrol key areas around your base and resource centers.

▼ At a Protoss base, take out Pylons near Gateways and Stargates first. The buildings lose power and become useless. Beware, however, of Probes that probably will scoot out to warp in new Pylons.

▼ Build plenty of defensive structures around your base(s). Zealots can make dog meat out of a lone Sunken Colony quickly, so always cross-protect your Colonies with at least two other units.

▼ Against Carriers, nothing can beat the Scourges' attack. A group of 12 Scourges can take out a Carrier in a few seconds, so always keep a group of inexpensive Scourges lying in wait.

▼ If any Arbiters come your way, have your Queens use Ensnare on units that might be hiding under the Arbiter's cloak.

Fig. 3-6. Scourges are an inexpensive and effective way to deal with Carriers.

Protoss

Technologically, the Protoss are the most highly evolved species. As such, they require special consideration when facing off against the other species. Because of the high cost of all Protoss units, you can't expect to win a war of attrition. Instead, you must do the most damage possible with the powerful Protoss units you have.

The Protoss actually have three new units they can produce in *Brood War*, but only two—the Dark Archon and the Corsair—are truly new. The Dark Templar were in the original *Starcraft*, but were special, unproducable units.

General Strategies and Tips

▼ For the Protoss, base layout is key. Place your Pylons so they power your buildings but don't clutter your base, and put important tech-tree structures close together in a very protected area.

▼ Protoss Probes needn't wait around to "build" a structure. They can simply open the Warp Rift and move on. This allows you to use all but one of your Probes for harvesting resources.

▼ Gas it up! More than any other species, the Protoss rely on Vespene Gas to build their high-priced units. Move to secure multiple Vespene Geysers whenever possible, or you may end up sucking fumes.

▼ Although Photon Cannons are an excellent defensive unit, they're fairly expensive. Build them in groups so they can support one another; then make sure to build more than one Pylon to service them. As a rule of thumb, build two Pylons for every three Photon Cannons.

▼ Have an Arbiter follow a unit in the group it's covering with its cloak. This way the Arbiter, although never actively engaged in battle, will follow just behind the attack force.

▼ Use the Templars' Hallucination ability: When attacking any large force, keep a good mix of hallucinated units in your front line. The enemy will waste many defensive attacks on units that don't exist.

▼ Throw a Templar or two in a Shuttle and move them to an area just behind an enemy mineral field. Then have your Templars use Psionic Storm on the streams of enemy workers approaching to collect resources. It's underhanded, but it works.

▼ Put an Observer over each unowned mineral field. When the enemy comes to set up a base, you'll know, and can take it out before it gets established.

▼ Fly an Arbiter behind enemy lines and have it use its Recall ability to bring in a group of Archons. Sit back and survey the carnage.

▼ If you use Carriers, make sure you upgrade their capacity before you take them into battle. The difference between a nonupgraded Carrier and an upgraded one is considerable, so it's worth waiting until you've completed that technological advance.

▼ The Dark Archon's Mind Control ability is perhaps the most powerful in the game. If you keep a group of four or so Dark Archons handy, you can use Mind Control to influence entire waves of enemy units and augment your own army.

▼ When using Mind Control, target units that are more powerful. Carriers and Battlecruisers are obvious choices, but any unit-carrying transport unit is great to capture. If you use Mind Control on a Dropship full of units, you gain control of not only the Dropship, but all the units *inside* it, as well.

▼ Use the Corsair's Disruption Web to blanket enemy Turrets/Photon Cannons/Spore Colonies; then use Carriers or Scouts to destroy them. Any unit under a Disruption Web is crippled and can't attacked, but they can still *be* attacked from the air.

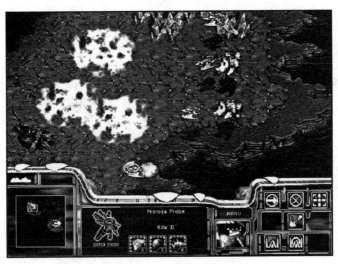

Fig. 3-7. The Corsair's Disruption Web is a very powerful tool for taking out enemy air defenses.

Against the Terrans

▼ Large groups of Carriers are very powerful, but keep an Observer with your Carrier groups so you can spot cloaked Wraiths.

▼ In multiplayer games, be ready for the Firebat rush. A combination of Zealots, Dragoons, and Photon Cannons are your best defense early on. Zealots alone generally are insufficient.

▼ Zealots are your best unit against Goliaths, but make sure they have their Speed upgrade before you try to chase one down. As with nearly all units, it's important to attack in force when pitting Zealots against Goliaths.

▼ Beware of pesky Science Vessels. An EMP used properly against your forces can rob you of your shields (until they regenerate). Spread out your units a little.

▼ Use a Carrier–Scout combination against Battlecruisers, and try to outnumber them. Ideally, you'll get a couple Arbiters to cloak your units while you attack.

▼ Keep a couple of Observers patrolling the base perimeter to check for cloaked Wraiths or Ghosts preparing to use Nukes.

▼ Using your Dark Archons to mind-control Battlecruisers can quickly turn the tide of battle. If you mind-control a Battlecruiser that's upgraded to the Yamato Cannon, you get to keep that upgrade!

Fig. 3-8. A group of Dark Archons can take control of small groups of enemy units in a few seconds.

Against the Zerg

▼ Build Dragoons to chase Zerg Overlords away from your base. Photon Cannons aren't always effective for this, because the Overlords will simply fly out of range. Never let enemies know anything they don't have to know.

▼ Zerglings can destroy Photon Cannons quickly, so make sure you have other troops handy to support your cannons in the face of an all-out rush.

▼ Try to keep an eye on all the units in your base. If a unit has caught a Parasite, use it against the enemy. For example, if a Zealot has been infested, send it (with a few other units) to attack an auxiliary Zerg target (such as a small outpost), and send your *real* attack force to the main Hive. Often the Zerg will pull their defenses toward the outpost, leaving the real target vulnerable.

▼ Build plenty of Dragoons and Scouts to defend against Mutalisks. If a large group of them attacks, counterattack in greater force, or you may lose your troops. Reavers are fantastic for attacking Zerg bases. Their Scarabs can decimate the smaller, more efficient Zerg bases quickly.

▼ If the enemy is using a lot of Zerglings against you, counter with Zealots. The Zerglings' small size makes them difficult to target, so use Attack–Move commands to put the Zealots in mop-up mode.

▼ Scourges make Carriers a bad investment against the Zerg. A Carrier can cost up to 950 in resources and can be destroyed by as few as five or six Scourge. That's a tough trade.

▼ Zerg bases often have plenty of Spore Colonies lining the perimeter. Use the Corsair's Disruption Web in conjunction with a group of Scouts to punch a hole in the Zerg air defense network.

Fig. 3-9. Zealots are as effective as any unit against Zerglings.

The Protoss Missions

The battle against the Zerg seemed to be over after Tassadar's heroic efforts at the end of *Starcraft*. It looked like the Protoss people could finally return to an existence unmarred by the bloody scourge of war. Unfortunately, the elimination of the Zerg was nothing more than wishful thinking; the Protoss will have to prove once again that they can overcome the Zerg menace.

Mission 1: Escape from Aiur

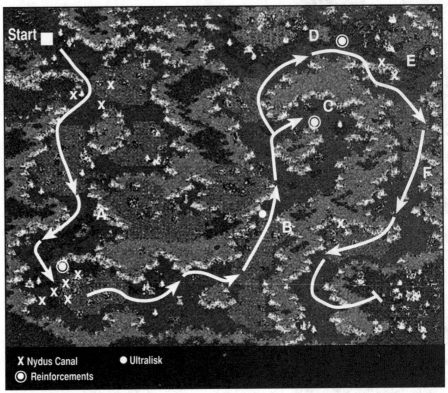

Fig. 4-1. Map of Protoss Mission 1

The evil Zerg Overmind has been destroyed and the Protoss home world of Aiur lies in ruins. As Executor of the remaining Protoss Forces, you must attempt to reunite your people and save them from the relentless Zerg forces. Your goal is to get Zeratul to the Warp Gate so he can lead the Protoss survivors to safety.

Mission Objectives

▼ Get Zeratul to the Warp Gate.
▼ Zeratul must survive.

Special Units

Zeratul (Dark Templar)

Battle Strategy

Your troops begin this mission in the upper-left corner of the map and include Zeratul (a Dark Templar), a group of Zealots, and a pair of Dragoons. For now, don't worry about grouping your units. Your first foray into enemy territory will require muscle more than finesse. This map is full of Nydus Canals. Unless destroyed, these will pump a limitless stream of Zerg units right to your team's doorstep.

CAUTION

Zeratul is invisible to most enemy units, but not to Spore Colonies and Overminds. Unfortunately, plenty of Overminds patrol this map, and you can bet there are Spore Colonies on those ridges just out of your view. Be careful with Zeratul: even *he* can be cut to pieces if the enemy spots him.

Although Zeratul is invisible to all but detector units (Spore Colonies, Overminds), you really can't take advantage of this ability. Vast numbers of Overmind detector units prowl this map.

Instead of using stealth, send your units into a bloodbath on the other side of the bridge. Have your units stand ready for general attacks while you use Zeratul's very powerful attack to destroy each Canal with a few quick swipes of his blade. In fact, Zeratul can take out all three Nydus Canals and a Sunken Colony while your other units mop up the few Zerg that pop out through the Nydus Canals.

Fig. 4-2. Charge this first set of Nydus Canals with everything you've got.

CAUTION

Numerous Sunken Colonies overlook your pathway from the ridges above. Often a few can strike you at once, so be ready to turn and run if you expect to be pile-driven by multiple Sunken Colonies.

Tackle the next leg of your long journey through this map quickly and aggressively. Move rapidly through the narrow canyon ahead because it houses a Sunken Colony. Move directly to Checkpoint A (see figure 4-1) as fast as possible.

When you reach this area, two Zealots will encourage you to follow them into battle. Do it. You'll come to a group of Zealots furiously fighting a large Zergling swarm in front of five (count 'em) Nydus Canals and a Sunken Colony. The troops fighting the Zerglings can manage them on their own, so set your troops to destroying the Nydus Canals as fast as they can. The longer you wait, the more Zerg troops will pour through the Canals, so get to it!

In the meantime, have Zeratul take out the Sunken Colony so your other troops can concentrate on the Canals and Zerglings. When the dust settles, you should have more troops than you started with.

The next area can be tricky, because it's guarded by Sunken Colonies in the pass. Again, be aggressive, especially with your newly acquired units. Charge up to Checkpoint B (see figure 4-1), destroying Zerg defenses as you go. You'll lose a few units, but your overwhelming numbers will take you to victory with minimal bloodshed.

Continue moving up the map to Checkpoint C (see figure 4-1), where, again, you'll collect new units after disposing of another Ultralisk.

Your goal now is to move up to Checkpoint D, where you'll meet a group of reinforcements that include Templars, Zealots, and even an Archon. As a bonus, you'll find Shield Batteries to charge up your unit's damaged shields. The next checkpoint area has a Nydus Canal and many, many burrowed Hydralisks. The key to getting past this area is to use your Templars to cast Psionic Storms around the Nydus Canal, and then rush the area with all your troops. That is, spray the area around the Nydus Canal with three or four hits of Psionic Storm, and then take out the Nydus Canal before more Hydralisks show up.

Fig. 4-3. Recharge your units' damaged shields using these Shield Batteries.

Proceed to the area above Checkpoint F, but don't rush into the canyon just yet. A pair of Sunken Colonies guard this canyon, and there are burrowed Zerglings and Hydralisks, as well; again, use your Templars' Psionic Storm ability to clear out as many burrowed Zerg as you can before rushing in to take out the Sunken Colonies. If you don't want to take out the Sunken Colonies around Checkpoint F, simply run past this area as fast as possible. However, an Ultralisk awaits you just down the canyon at Checkpoint G, so you may want to take it a little slower and destroy every enemy unit you encounter as you work down toward the Warp Gate.

When you face off against the Checkpoint G Ultralisk, you can storm it with everything you've got or soften it up with a couple of Psionic Storms before rushing in. Either way, you must destroy these Ultralisks before you

can proceed. The Warp Gate is very close, and the path is mostly clear. You still have some burrowed Zerglings to deal with, but at this point simply run Zeratul up to the beacon to claim victory.

Fig. 4-4. When you reach this point, just run Zeratul up to the Warp Gate and victory will be yours.

Resource Management

No resource management is really involved in this mission. Instead, you'll simply manage the forces you start with, and later the units you get as reinforcements. Don't be afraid to sacrifice a unit or two to lure the enemy into a trap (using Psionic Storms or Dragoons). You'll receive a decent number of reinforcements over the course of this mission, so one or two sacrificed Zealots won't turn the tide. You also should take full advantage of the Shield Batteries near Checkpoint D, especially if you have many units with heavily damaged shields.

Mission 2: Dunes of Shakuras

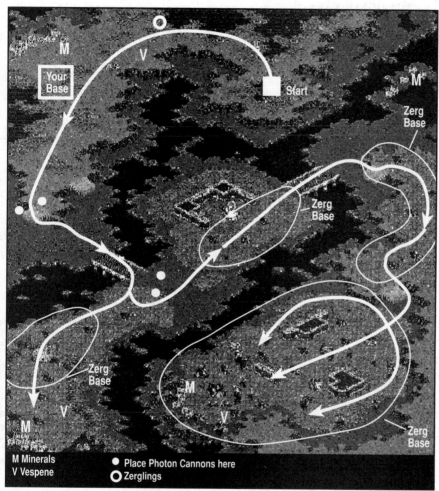

Fig. 4-5. Map of Protoss Mission 2

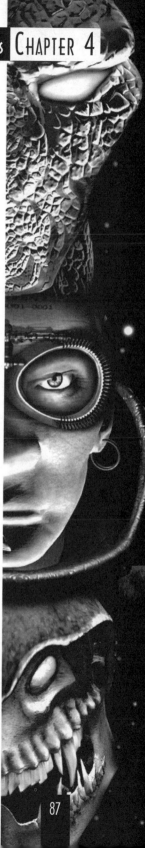

Your troops have made it through the Warp Gate to the world of Shakuras, where you hope to find an area suitable for establishing a settlement.

When you begin to explore Shakuras, however, you soon realize the Zerg have found their way to this Dark Templar home world. Now you must try to eliminate the Zerg presence. Fortunately, you'll have the help of some Dark Templars.

Mission Objectives

▼ Build a base including Nexus, Gateway, and Stargate.
▼ Destroy the Zerg Base.

Special Units

None

Battle Strategy

You begin this mission with Zealots and Probes in the upper-central map area. You must move your units to the mineral field in the map's upper-left corner, but expect to meet Zerglings along the way. Once you've made it to the mineral field, build a Nexus and get the ball rolling by harvesting minerals.

Your first defensive priorities involve putting up a few Photon Cannons around the mineral field. The Zerg will launch a pile of Zerglings at you as soon as you begin to get established, but a few Dark Templars will show up to lend a hand. Your goal now is simply to hunker down and protect your assets while you build up your resources.

Fig. 4-6. After building your Nexus, expect a Zergling attack. Four Dark Templars will help you, however.

CAUTION

In this mission, the Zerg menace attacks your forces in wave after wave. Your base in the upper-left corner will take multiple attacks from both air and ground, so be ready, even if you've expanded to other areas.

After establishing your base, place a series of Photon Cannons near the ramps to the south (see figure 4-5) to stem the tide of Zerg attacks and allow you to build up structures and technologies. Then you must take at least one of the two other major resource fields before taking on the main Zerg Base. I suggest the area in the map's lower-left corner, because it makes a good staging area for your eventual attack on the main Zerg base.

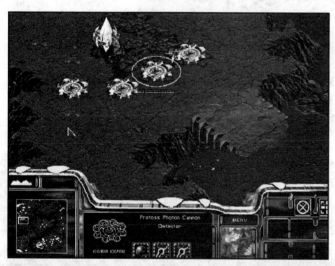

Fig. 4-7. A layer of Photon Cannons goes a long way to protect your main base.

TIP

Always try to acquire all upgrades (especially plasma shields) before attempting to launching a major attack into enemy territory.

After taking your second mineral field, build a Nexus and some Photon Cannons to protect it. Then begin building an attack force to mount the assault on the main Zerg base—12 Zealots, 12 Dragoons, and at least two Reavers (three or four would be better). Then systematically move this force toward the main Zerg base. Lead with your Reavers, which will take out Sunken Colonies with just three Scarab hits. Keep your Dragoons close by to fend off Mutalisk attacks; likewise, keep your Zealots nearby in case you run into a Zergling swarm.

Continue moving toward the Zerg base this way (leading with your Reavers), supplying your Reavers continually with fresh Scarabs. You'll handily destroy one Zerg structure after another until their entire base is decimated. Once the structures are gone, you win the mission. You needn't destroy every Zerg unit, just the structures.

Fig. 4-8. A balanced force of Reavers, Zealots, and Dragoons will help you crush the Zerg menace.

Strategy Counterpoint

Blizzard quality assurance analyst John Lagrave has different ideas about which units to use to attack the Zerg base. He suggests Dragoons and Dark Templars: the Dark Templars are invisible to all Zerg units except Spore Colonies and Overlords. Lagrave sends in Dragoons to take out these detector units so the Dark Templars can rip Zerg structures to shreds unseen.

Resource Management

For your assault on the Zerg base to succeed, you must upgrade your technologies to their maximum settings. Therefore, you must take at least one of the two extra mineral/Vespene locations. Which you take is your choice, although the area on the right side of the map lacks a Vespene Geyser. Structure and technological development shouldn't come before basic defenses, so keep plenty of Zealots, Dragoons, and the odd Photon Cannon standing by for the waves of attacking enemies. Spending some resources on defense early on will save you resources later.

Mission 3: Legacy of the Xel'Naga

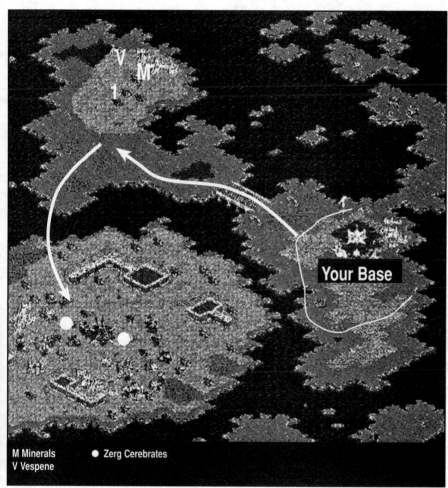

M Minerals ● Zerg Cerebrates
V Vespene

Fig. 4-9. Map of Protoss Mission 3

Raszagal, Matriarch of the Dark Templar, tells of an ancient edifice known as the Xel'Naga Temple. Dedicated to the forerunners of the Protoss species, the temple stands near a nexus of powerful cosmic energies that may help in the fight against the Zerg. Unfortunately, the Broods of two nearby Cerebrates guard the sacred structure, and you must destroy them if you're ever to reclaim the temple of the Xel'Naga.

Mission Objectives

▼ Destroy the Zerg Cerebrates.

Special Units

Zerg Cerebrates

Battle Strategy

You begin with a sizable base in the central-right area of the map, with plenty of Zerg activity nearby in the lower-left corner. There are two main resource areas to exploit (and you'll probably have to) in this mission, but first, you should build at least four Photon Cannons at the south end of your base while you build up your structures and technology.

Fig. 4-10. A few attacks are likely to come from the south, so place a Photon Cannon or two for backup.

Just after the mission begins, you'll get help from four Shuttles and four Corsairs moving to take Resource Area 1 (see figure 4-9). Concentrate the firepower of the four Dragoons dropped into Area 1 to take out the Sunken Colony and any Zerg units that happen by. After toasting the Zerg structures, move your Dark Templars and one Probe to the area and have your Probe construct a Nexus. Be sure to build a pair of Pylons and several Photon Cannons south of the minerals to help fend off occasional Zerg attacks.

This mission affords you plenty of minerals, so build plenty of Photon Cannons to guard your two bases. The money you spend on these cannons will pay off later, when you won't have to waste troops defending against random Zerg attacks.

Spend the time to climb the tech tree completely and upgrade all your units to the max. Then address your attack force: build at least six Scouts, four Corsairs, five Shuttles, and numerous ground forces, including Reavers, Zealots, Dragoons, and, most importantly, Dark Templars. Only Dark Templars can destroy Cerebrates, so don't skimp on these units. A coordinated air and ground attack, along with the Corsair's Disruption Web technology, will make killing the Cerebrates a lot easier than it would be with an unbalanced attack.

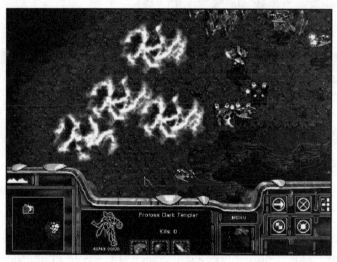

Fig. 4-11. Use Disruption Webs to clear a landing area for your Shuttles.

The Cerebrates are heavily guarded by Spore and Sunken colonies; using Disruption Webs and Scouts to take out Zerg defenses is your best bet. After you clear out Spore colonies on the Zerg frontier, it's safe for your Shuttles to land while your Scouts and Corsairs move in to wreak havoc. The Reavers will plow a quick pathway to the Cerebrate, where your Dark Templars must do the killing.

TIP

Remember, only Dark Templars can kill Cerebrates.

This mission is all about taking auxiliary resource areas while continually climbing the tech tree. Once you have the requisite units (Reavers, Corsairs, Dark Templars), move in and take on the large Zerg bases guarding the Cerebrates. After you vanquish both Cerebrates, victory is yours.

Fig. 4-12. Use Dark Templars to take out the Cerebrates.

Resource Management

This map is unique because you can gain access to all the resources you need simply by securing Area 1. If you're unsure whether you have the forces you need to move on a Cerebrate, then take time to harvest more resources. Time is on your side in this mission. The Zerg will continue to attack, but they're nothing a few carefully placed Photon Cannons can't handle.

The most important aspect of resource management here is to climb the entire tech tree and research all abilities so all your units are fully prepared to deal with the formidable Zerg forces.

Mission 4: The Quest for Uraj

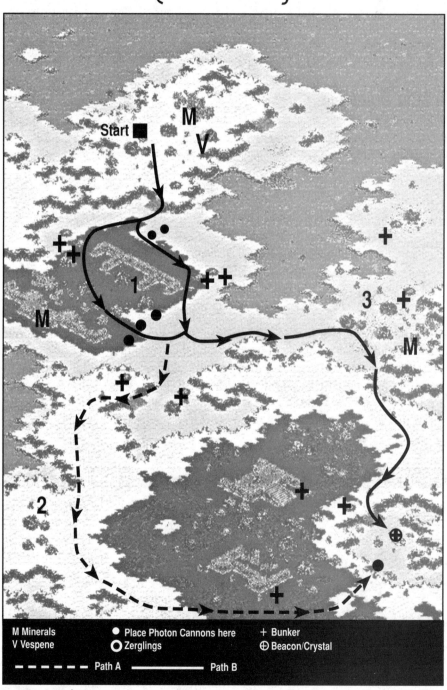

M Minerals	● Place Photon Cannons here + Bunker
V Vespene	◉ Zerglings ⊕ Beacon/Crystal

- - - - - Path A ——————— Path B

Fig. 4-13. Map of Mission 4

Kerrigan informs you that, because the Overmind is dead, she's no longer under Zerg control. She requests your help in gathering the two crystals—Uraj and Khalis. Raszagal tells you to put aside your ill feelings toward Kerrigan and accept her help in finding the Uraj Crystal.

Mission Objectives

▼ Take Kerrigan to the Uraj Crystal.
▼ Kerrigan must survive.

Special Units

Kerrigan

Battle Strategy

As this mission begins, three Shuttles drop three Reavers and three Dragoons smack-dab in the middle of a Terran base. Once the initial defenses are disabled, another Shuttle arrives with Kerrigan and four Probes. It's from these humble beginnings that you must build the forces necessary to get Kerrigan to the Uraj Crystal (in the map's lower-right corner). Once you get control of your units, the first thing you must do is finish clearing Terran structures from around the mineral field.

CAUTION

Beware the Bunker at the south end of the landing area; it can take you by surprise if you're not ready for it.

Fig. 4-14. Use your Reavers to take out these Bunkers easily.

As you establish your base, take your Reavers and relieve the Terrans of four of their Bunkers. They lie just down the ramp, and effectively defend Area 1. Three Reavers will do it, but make sure you're well-stocked with Scarabs.

After destroying the Bunkers, have Kerrigan cloak and take out the Siege Tank protecting Area 1. As soon as Kerrigan begins her attack, the Terrans will use a Comsat Station to scan the area, so after the Tank is destroyed get her out of there.

With the Siege Tank gone, the door is open for your Reavers and Dragoons to move in and crush the Terran base. Don't overextend yourself: move slowly and deliberately until you've cleared an area for building a new Nexus.

When the Terrans are gone, build some Pylons and Photon Cannons along the south edge of Area 1; this route will bring you plenty of visitors. After Area 1 is secure, start building a balanced force of air and ground units for your attack on the remaining Terran forces.

Fig. 4-15. To follow Path A, you must eliminate this Terran area.

You can approach this mission either with stealth or with brute force.

If you go down the left side of the map (Path A), you can sweep down and under the bulk of enemy forces with minimal fighting. You'll still have to deal with a few Bunkers and a Siege Tank or two. To make this approach work, you must move aggressively to take out Area 2. After eliminating Area 2 and the Missile Turrets north of it, you need only get past the bottleneck at the bottom of the map to reach the crystal.

Path A is a decent route if you've managed your resources well and are flush with "cash." But if you're running low, Path B is the way to go. This involves capturing Area 3 and plundering its resources before heading south to the crystal. To make this approach work, you must take Area 3 and destroy the Barracks to the north. Then use Dragoons to take out the Missile Turrets on the ridge south of Area 3. When two of these Turrets are gone, use your Shuttles to drop in a ground force that can easily clear the path to the crystal. I find this approach more satisfying than sneaking along Path A.

Once Kerrigan gets to the Crystal, you win the mission.

Fig. 4-16. The resources in Area 3 could be just what the doctor ordered if you've been too free with your resources.

Resource Management

As soon as the first area is secure, you must build a Nexus, Pylons, and an Assimilator to get started up your tech tree. You start with 1000 mineral units, and so have a solid head start on your base without having to spend time harvesting resources. There's no substitute for upgrading your units' abilities, so use the resources to do so and your life will be easier.

Capturing the starting base and Area 1 is mandatory, but Area 3 is optional. If you find yourself fighting defensively (and wasting resources) in the beginning of the mission, you may want to take Area 3 for its minerals. It's also important to guard your bases well with Photon Cannons right from the start; otherwise the Terran menace may get in and destroy some primary structures. Better safe than sorry.

Mission 5: The Battle of Braxis

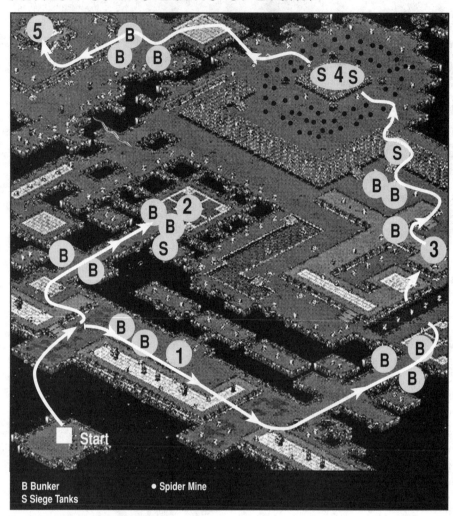

B Bunker
S Siege Tanks

● Spider Mine

Fig. 4-17. Map of Protoss Mission 5

The United Earth Directorate has taken control of the defense network on Braxis and is denying access to Artanis and the Protoss. Artanis won't be swayed in his desire to penetrate the defenses, and vows he'll find a way. The Protoss must disable the five generators that power the vast network of Missile Turrets if they have any hope of breaching Braxis's defenses.

Mission Objectives

▼ Destroy the five power generators to pierce the UED blockage.
▼ Artanis must survive.

Special Units

▼ Artanis (Scout)
▼ Power Generators

Battle Strategy

You must approach this mission one power generator at a time. After destroying each generator, you'll get a group of reinforcements ranging from Dark Templars to Reavers and Scouts.

There are several ways to approach this mission and several routes you can navigate successfully to take out all the generators. What follows is just one workable option.

To reach Power Generator 1 you must land your troops (via Shuttle) in the area left of the generator. From there, take out the nearby Missile Turrets using Zealots and Dragoons.

Next, you have two Bunkers to deal with. There are a couple of ways to take these out. Probably the best is just to use brute force and bring all your forces to bear on each Bunker, one at a time. If any units' shields get low, move them out of the area. Remember, shields can recover, but damaged units are damaged for good.

Fig. 4-18. Take out these Bunkers using brute force.

CAUTION

Attack each pesky Bunker from afar with Dragoons and Scouts. The units inside Bunkers usually will target just one of your units, so when a unit's shields get low, get it away so it takes no permanent damage. By rotating units this way, you can take out the Bunkers without lasting damage to your troops.

Destroying Power Generator 1 disabled enough Missile Turrets for you to move to Area A with your Shuttles. The key to taking out the Bunkers near Area A is to use your newly acquired Dark Templar reinforcements. The units in the Bunkers won't see the Dark Templars, so you'll make short work of them.

Use your Scouts to take out the Siege Tank northeast of the Bunkers you just destroyed (see figure 4-17). Next, creep toward Power Generator 2. Two Bunkers and several Missile Turrets guard this generator. A good way to succeed here is to storm the Bunkers and take them out as quickly as you can. Once the Bunkers are gone, you can destroy Generator 2 easily.

Fig. 4-19. Have your Dark Templars take out these Bunkers.

Now backtrack to the map's lower-right corner. From this position, work your way toward Generator 3, but you'll have the usual assortment of Bunkers and Siege Tanks to deal with. Use the same techniques to chip away at the Bunkers: Move Scouts or Dragoons up to pound the Bunkers into the red zone. (Once a Terran structure's health bar turns red, it will continue deteriorating until it's destroyed.) Remember to rotate out units with depleted shields. When you reach Area B, have your Dragoons take out the row of Missile Turrets blocking your path to Area C. At Area C, destroy the generator outright with your Dragoons from across the gap.

TIP

Beware of Siege Tanks lurking around this map. They'll toast your units before you know what's happening.

After you knock out Generator 3, Reaver and Templar reinforcements arrive. Both make capturing the next generator easier.

Move your Reavers to the edge of Area B to take out the Bunkers there. The Siege Tank up the ramp from Area B prevents you from reaching Generator 4; take it out with some quick, aggressive action. Run four Zealots up to the Siege Tank as fast as you can. They'll destroy it without taking undue damage.

Generator 4 poses a unique challenge. It's surrounded by Spider Mines, Missile Turrets, and Ghosts at the four corners. Adding insult to injury, two Siege Tanks and a pair of Goliaths sit right beside the generator. To get at the generator, you'll have to send at least a pair of Observers to locate the Spider Mines. Once they show where the mines are, your Dragoons can destroy the mines methodically from a distance and clear a path to the generator. The Templar's Psionic Storm also is an excellent weapon against Spider Mines. Use it to take out the Ghosts at the corners of the generator platform. Take care not to get too close to the platform or you'll get smoked by Siege Tank fire.

Fig. 4-20. Use Psionic Storm to clear a path to Generator 3.

After taking out the Missile Turrets along the path to the generator platform, load your Reavers and as many other ground units as you can muster onto Shuttles. Quickly move the Shuttles over the generator platform, and then drop all the units as fast as you can. If you do this fast enough, you probably won't lose a Shuttle; your Reavers will destroy the Siege Tanks almost immediately. The generator soon will follow.

TIP

Hide your units under the Arbiter you receive after you destroy Generator 4.

Approach the final generator (5 on the map) by dropping all your ground units at Area E. After you destroyed Generator 4 you received Corsairs, Scouts, and an Arbiter. Use your Arbiter as cover for your air units, and then have your Corsairs use Disruption Webs to incapacitate the various Missile Turrets standing between you and Generator 5.

Finally, drop all your ground troops near the generator and rush it with an all-out attack. Several Battlecruisers guard the generator, and unless they're checked, you'll fail miserably. Fortunately, you have an Arbiter at your disposal. If you take out at least two Battlecruisers with a Stasis attack, and use your Scouts to distract the Goliaths and any remaining Battlecruisers, you should be successful.

It may seem desperate to throw all your remaining forces at Generator 5, but once it's destroyed, you've won, whether you have half your units left or only Artanis.

Resource Management

No true resource management is involved in this mission. This becomes all too apparent when you go to build Scarabs for your Reavers only to find that you have no minerals. Instead of harvesting resources, you'll manage only unit resources. You can count on reinforcements after you destroy each generator, but if you lose too many units in any one leg of the mission you may come up short when you need units later on.

Don't be foolhardy with the units you get. As you attack each generator, keep in mind you must try to make your current units last the whole mission. This attitude will put you in good stead for the final assault on Generator 5.

Mission 6: Return to Char

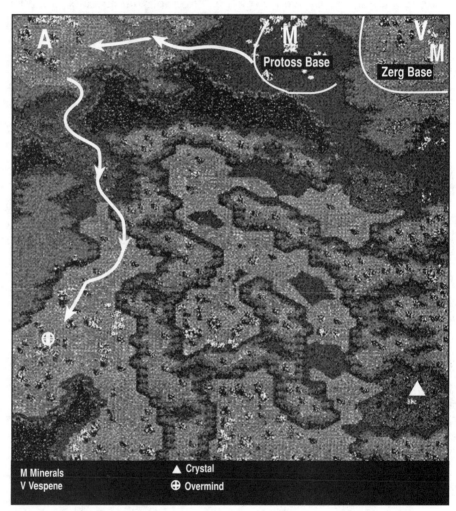

Fig. 4-21. Map of Protoss Mission 6

The Zerg Overmind has nested near your objective—the Khalis Crystal. As you plan a way to directly retrieve the Crystal, Artanis suggests that if enough damage can be done to the Overmind, the surrounding Zerg may be pacified to the point where the Khalis Crystal will be easy to retrieve. Either way, the Crystal must be recovered.

Mission Objectives

Retrieve the Khalis Crystal *or* do enough damage to the Overmind to send it into remission.

Special Units

▼ Zerg Overmind

Battle Strategy

This mission may overwhelm at first glance: The entire map is infested with Zerg Spore Colonies and Scourge units. Thus, a direct air attack isn't a good idea. Instead, use large numbers of basic warriors to clear a path to your objective and wreak havoc. Because the Zerg Overmind is less heavily defended than the Khalis Crystal, make it your primary target.

You begin with a Zerg camp in the map's upper-right corner and a Protoss camp left of it, in the upper-central area. The Zerg camp is vulnerable to ground attack from the south, so position your first Sunken Colonies and Zerglings immediately south of the camp. The Protoss camp is vulnerable to attack from the southeast, so station your first Defenders in the narrow pass below and right of the camp.

Use your Dark Templars to defend your camp. Build Photon Cannons along the south side of the Protoss base: Zerg Mutalisks and occasional groups of Zerglings and Hydralisks will attack regularly from the air. Don't venture your units too far south of your camps, lest they awaken waiting Zerg forces.

Fig. 4-22. Build up a healthy arsenal of Photon Cannons with which to defend your base.

The best way to reach the Overmind (in the lower-left corner of the map) is to capture the resources in Area A and then fight your way south. Build up a force of Zealots, Dragoons, Zerglings, and Hydralisks and station them left of the Protoss camp. Don't let them ascend the ramp to the higher plateau; Zerg Lurkers wait here. Be sure to take along an Observer when you're ready to attack the Zerg camp in the map's upper-left corner.

After clearing the enemy Zerg camp in the upper-left corner, establish your own Zerg base there. You could build a Protoss camp, but Zerg units are cheaper and you can build up a camp and its defenses faster with them. Start marshaling warriors immediately south of the new Zerg base for your final attack on the enemy Overmind.

A path leads south from your new base in Area A to the Overmind. You must clear and follow this route. It opens into a large enemy Zerg camp well-defended by Queens, Spore Colonies, Sunken Colonies, and Lurkers. Accompany your forces with Protoss Observers, steering clear of enemy detector units along the plateaus overlooking your path to the Overmind.

The paltry few Observers with which you start the level are insufficient to guide your forces for the entire battle, so build a Protoss Robotics Facility and an Observatory before starting your final attack. Dragoons are critical to your success, as well, because they can attack the Zerg Queens waiting to defend the Overmind. Equal numbers of Zealots and Dragoons, Zerglings and Hydralisks, make an effective force if you send your Observers along.

Build warriors constantly at both Zerg Hive Clusters and the Protoss base to reinforce depleted troops attacking the Overmind. Constructing a second Gateway in your Protoss base will speed the buildup.

Because the path from your second Zerg base to the Overmind is narrow, move only one group of units through at a time. This renders them vulnerable to attack, so explore cautiously.

Fig. 4-23. There are plenty of Lurkers around the Overmind, so be sure to bring Observers with you.

You needn't wipe out the entire Zerg camp around the Overmind to win. You need only clear a path through to it and wear it down by attacking it repeatedly. Fortunately, most enemy forces will ignore you as long as they don't see you, so keep your units tightly together and make sure they don't go wandering off after peripheral attackers on your path to the Overmind.

Destroy enemy Queens when they appear; they're very damaging and can strike from afar. Keep Dragoons and Hydralisks in good supply even after you start attacking the Overmind.

Resource Management

Sufficient resources to complete the mission are available at the two camps where you begin—if you can capture the area's third resource node. The Protoss have no nearby Vespene Geyser, so the Zerg Refinery in the upper-right corner must supply all necessary Vespene until you establish the second base in the upper left. You'll probably deplete all the minerals and Vespene at your first Zerg camp before the mission ends.

Concentrate your resources on creating large numbers of basic ground units. This way you avoid depleting your cache of crystals and gas on expensive units that won't fare well against the heavily fortified Zerg forces infesting virtually the entire map.

Mission 7: The Insurgent

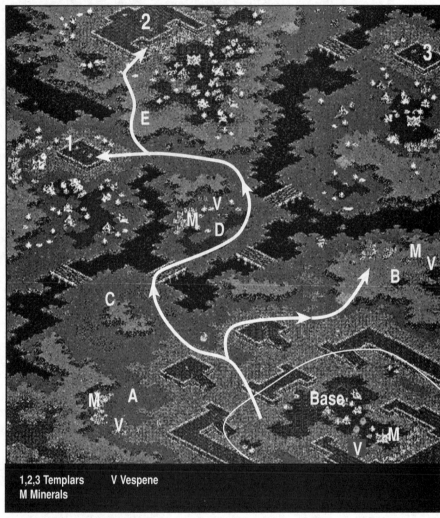

1,2,3 Templars   V Vespene
M Minerals

Fig. 4-24. Map of Protoss Mission 7

Judicator Aldaris and a legion of Khalai survivors from Aiur have begun an open revolt against the remaining Protoss forces. Aldaris and his troops feel it was wrong to abandon Aiur for Shakuras, and even now they prepare an attack on your forces. You must find Aldaris and destroy him if you hope to stem this tide of dissent.

Mission Objectives

▼ Kill the traitor Aldaris.

Special Units

Aldaris (High Templar)

Battle Strategy

The key to this mission lies in your Dark Archons' ability to use Mind Control to capture enemy units. Each of three platforms holds someone who looks like the High Templar Aldaris; only one is real. The others are hallucinations. To win, you must kill or mind-control the real Aldaris. All-out aggression pays off in this mission. The longer you sit back and try to build up your defenses, the more enemy attacks you'll endure.

Immediately take your two Dark Archons, a Probe, and a pair of Dark Templars to Area C. Along the way you may run into an enemy unit or two; simply use Mind Control to beef up your forces. At Area C, build a pair of Pylons, and then secure the leftmost bridge with a row of Photon Cannons. Securing this area will stop 50 percent of the enemy attacks on your base early in the game.

Fig. 4-25. Securing this bridge early on saves you plenty of trouble later.

Your next goal should be Area D. Several enemy Photon Cannons and Pylons stand in your way there, and usually a small contingent of Zealots shows up to stem your attack. Move a group of Zealots into the area to take out the Photon Cannons, while your Dark Archons mind-control any enemy Zealots that enter.

After taking Area D, branch out and build a Nexus in areas A and B, where there are plenty of minerals and Vespene to harvest.

TIP

Use your Mind Control ability on units that really count, such as loaded Shuttles or Carriers.

You've gained control of this map's key areas. Now you can spend time and resources upgrading your units' shields and abilities. The enemy boasts the maximum in all upgrades and abilities, so you must, too, if you're to combat them effectively. Build up a force of at least eight Dark Archons (it's nice to keep four on the front lines and four in the back, usually recharging). This arrangement means you'll always have the ability to mind-control an enemy unit when you need it.

TIP

The Shield Battery is also extremely effective in getting your Dark Archons' defenses back up quickly, as they burn through all of their shields when using Mind Control.

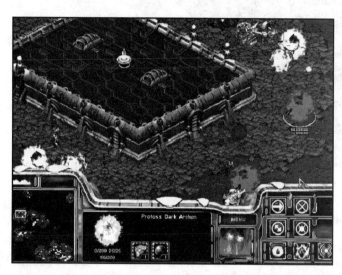

Fig. 4-26. Killing Templar 1 is good practice for the real thing. Aldaris is Templar 2 on the map.

Build up a force of ground units to escort a group of several Dark Archons, and then go after Templar 1. Although Templar 1 is nothing more than a hallucination, it's good practice to get your troops close enough for your Archons to mind-control him. To do this, move your ground units in to take out the Photon Cannons while your Dark Archons hang back and get ready to mind-control any enemy units threatening your Archons. Save one Dark Archon for the Mind Control on Templar 1. Simply move close to the platform and use the Mind Control ability on the Templar.

The *real* Aldaris is Templar 2 (see figure 4-24), so if you just go after that area, you can win a little quicker. To get to Aldaris, drop a large force of ground units, with at least four Dark Archons, into Area E, a small peninsula unprotected by Photon Cannons. When the enemy senses your arrival, he'll throw everything he's got at you, including Carriers. Use your Dark Archons to mind-control the Carriers and increase your chances of surviving your first attack wave. You may have to make several Shuttle drops on Area E before you can get close to the real Aldaris. After you kill Aldaris, Kerrigan shows up and the mission ends.

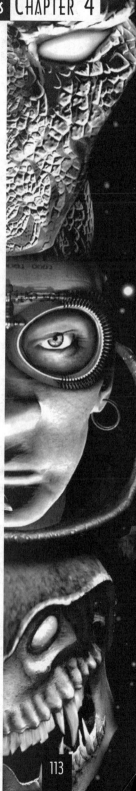

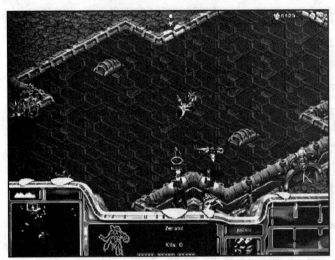

Fig. 4-27. After you finally kill or mind-control Aldaris, Kerrigan shows up to generate her own brand of trouble.

Resource Management

Begin harvesting resources as soon as the mission begins. However, the real harvesting will occur after you've secured areas C and D. Once you've secured your front line of defenses, immediately branch out and build a Nexus in areas A, B, and D. Harvest resources as fast as you can, so you can climb the tech tree quickly. The enemy is already equipped with maximum upgrades and abilities, so your units won't be able to fight them effectively until you've upgraded them to the max. Fortunately, there are plenty of resources to help you achieve this. You just have to make sure to bottleneck the enemy's attack routes in areas D and C.

Mission 8: Countdown

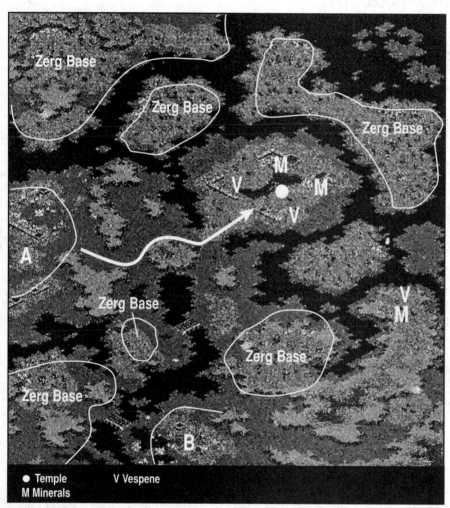

Fig. 4-28. Map of Protoss Mission 8

The time to crush the Zerg offensive is upon you. You must have Artanis and Zeratul take the Uraj and Khalis Crystals to the beacon near the Xel'Naga Temple. In the 15 minutes before the temple's power is unleashed, the Zerg surely will mount an all-out attack on it, so be prepared for the battle of a lifetime.

Mission Objectives

▼ Take Artanis and Zeratul to the temple.
▼ Artanis and Zeratul must survive.
▼ Protect the temple from the Zerg assault.

Special Units

Xel'Naga Temple

Battle Strategy

You begin the mission with two Protoss bases in areas A and B. From these two bases, you must mount an attack on Area C (Xel'Naga Temple). However, before you move to recapture the temple, you must build up a solid ground force of Zealots and Dragoons (and maybe a few Photon Cannons) to protect your existing bases, because the Zerg will launch attacks periodically on both areas.

TIP

Build Shield Batteries near the perimeters of your bases so your defending troops can recharge their shields quickly and easily.

As in the last mission, it helps a great deal if you can upgrade your units as the mission progresses. But don't put all your resources into upgrades: divide them up to build an attack force for taking the temple. Once you have a group of Dragoons, Zealots, and a few Reavers, move (along the ground) toward the temple, taking out Sunken Colonies and enemy units as you go. You meet some light resistance at the temple, but as long as you have a few Dragoons for air cover, your Reavers can do most of your ground work.

Fig. 4-29. Take the temple area using a combination of Reavers and Dragoons.

At the temple, you must work quickly to build a Nexus so you can begin harvesting the vast nearby mineral resources. Place Pylons around the entry points to the temple area so you can set out a protective grid of Photon Cannons. To be safe, lay down lines of Photon Cannons one or two deep, with ground units nearby to back them up. Surrounding the temple with Photon Cannons is expensive, but the Zerg will hit you with a huge onslaught once the crystals are on the Beacon, so you won't be sorry.

NOTE

Build a Gateway inside the temple area so you can produce ground units quickly when you need them.

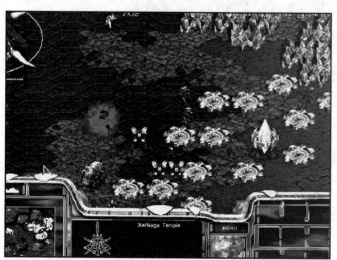

Fig. 4-30. Don't be afraid to build up a large defense force around the temple. The Zerg attack is formidable.

117

Once your base is built up around the temple, you can bring Artanis and Zeratul to the Beacon. This starts a 15-minute countdown during which *all* your bases will fall under attack—none more than the temple area.

Although you have Photon Cannons defending the temple area already, you should have plenty of Dragoons to deal with enemy air units that get past your perimeter defenses. Likewise, a group of Scouts goes a long way toward eliminating the threat of Guardians breaking your defensive line. It's a good idea to keep a Reaver at each temple entrance, as well, in case a group of Zerglings manages to get past your Cannons.

CAUTION

Keep a Dark Archon or two inside the temple area so you can mind-control Zerg Overlords that carry units to drop into the fray.

The Zerg onslaught lasts for 15 minutes. If you defend with ground troops and Photon Cannons, you should have no problem holding them off.

The fly in the ointment is the Zerg's packs of Guardians, there to take out your Photon Cannons. The Guardians' longer range will render you helpless unless you have Scouts or Dragoons handy. Carriers aren't usually recommended in this level, because the Zerg send in waves of Scourge that destroy Carriers quickly.

After the timer runs down to zero, victory is yours.

Fig. 4-31. The Zerg like to use Guardians to destroy your defenses from afar, so keep some Scouts around to defend against them.

Resource Management

Use your original bases' resources aggressively: once you've taken the temple area, you'll have plenty of minerals and Vespene to work with. Spend as many resources as it takes to climb the tech tree and give your units all available upgrades and abilities. In particular, make sure your shields are upgraded to the maximum setting.

When you're ready to begin the final battle, you can sacrifice your Probes, so you'll have more Psi available for military units. In this mission, it's not uncommon to build up to the 200 unit Psi limit.

he Terran Missions

United Earth Directorate has sent its greatest military leader, Admiral Gerard
alle, to capture the new Zerg Overmind and bend its minions to the sovereign
of humanity. Fighting other Terrans won't be easy or palatable, but it's necessary
he new Zerg Overmind is to be kept in check.

Mission 1: First Strike

Fig. 5-1. Map of Terran Mission 1

The UED has arrived at Braxis, an outlying Dominion stronghold. You must assault the outpost on Braxis and secure the planet for UED forces. To capture the outpost, you must destroy the Command Center in the main base, but you'll have help in your efforts from Samir Duran and his Confederate Resistance forces (which you'll meet along the way).

Mission Objectives

▼ Destroy the enemy Command Center.

Special Units

Duran (Ghost)

Battle Strategy

This mission begins in the lower-left corner of the map, and, although you have plenty of minerals at your disposal, you don't have a lick of Vespene. Build up a force of ten Marines and two Tanks (which you start with, anyway) and move quickly up to Area 1. Take out the enemy units in Area 1, and be sure to destroy the Barracks there so the enemy can't build new units from that location. After cleaning out Area 1, head up to Duran's camp.

Fig. 5-2. Take out the Barracks in Area 1 as soon as you have a small attack force ready.

At Duran's camp Duran (a Ghost) and his forces offer to help. This is a boon: you obtain a second base without having to build it yourself; plus, Duran's forces have a Vespene Geyser, which you desperately need. Research

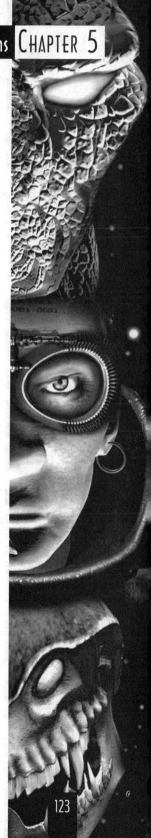

the Siege Tank ability, and then place three tanks and four Goliaths near Area 2. These units can fend off all air and ground attacks the enemy sends through that area.

Fig. 5-3. Set up some Siege Tanks with Goliaths as backup in Area 2.

After Area 2 is secured, your goal is only to climb the tech tree and upgrade all your units as you build a force of four or five Siege Tanks, a dozen Marines, and about 10 Goliaths. When you're ready, take this force up to Area 3 and destroy the Barracks there. As you get close to Area 3, you'll face waves of attacks from the enemy base, but you can deal with these if you simply set up your Siege Tanks with your Marines as backup. If any enemy Dropships or Wraiths come by, your Goliaths will shred them.

Leave a few forces behind to distract the enemy at its base exit near Area 3, and move your main body of forces up to Area 4, the base's "back door." This will allow you to catch onrushing enemy troops in a bottleneck in the mineral field. Four Siege Tanks and a group of Marines will kick butt. Remember, you need only destroy the Terran Command Center, which is very close to Area 4, so inch your Siege Tanks forward until they can take the Command Center out and victory will be yours.

Fig. 5-4. Follow Duran's suggestion and attack the Command Center from the "back door" near Area 4.

Resource Management

Immediately set your SCVs to harvesting minerals, and build five more SCVs to keep minerals flowing in the first part of this mission. Once they're all harvesting full-bore, you can devote your resources to building the Marines you'll need to get to Duran's Vespene.

After assimilating Duran's camp, get the Vespene you need to repair units and research Siege Tanks. If you find yourself in need of more minerals, exploit the lightly defended mineral field in the middle of the left side of the map, but you should have more than enough resources between your original base and Duran's base to make this mission a success.

Mission 2: The Dylarian Shipyards

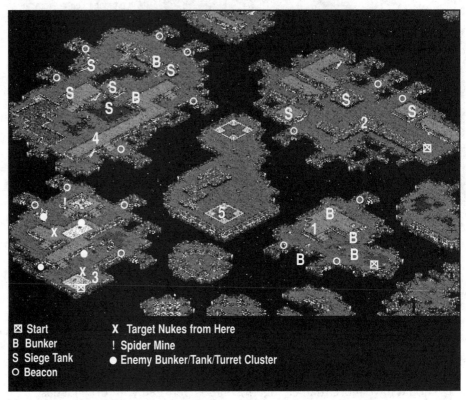

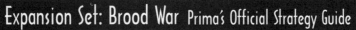

⊠ Start	X Target Nukes from Here
B Bunker	! Spider Mine
S Siege Tank	● Enemy Bunker/Tank/Turret Cluster
O Beacon	

Fig. 5-5. Map of Terran Mission 2

Although Dugalle was impressed with Duran's work, he doubts Duran's loyalty. In any case, Duran has provided valuable tactical information for a mission at the Dylarian shipyards, which house a number of functional Battlecruisers for the Dominion. Your job is to capture as many of the capital ships as you can. When the Battlecruisers are yours, crush the Dominion forces.

Mission Objectives

▼ Steal Battlecruisers
▼ Defeat the Dominion strike force.

Special Units

Terran Pilots

Battle Strategy

As the mission begins, three Dropships deposit your Marines, Medics, and Pilots in Area 1. Only Bunkers of Marines and Firebats guard the beacons here, so don't worry about Siege Tanks taking out your entire force.

Move your Marines and Medics in force against each successive Bunker. The enemy will wound your Marines, but your Medics will heal them as fast as they take damage. This Medic–Marine combination will make this area easy to secure.

After destroying all the Bunkers, send each Pilot to a beacon.

Fig. 5-6. Use a Marine–Medic combination to take out the Bunkers in Area 1.

In Area 2, be wary of three Siege Tanks guarding each beacon. The Tanks are on platforms, out of your visual and attack range, but you have two very effective ways of dealing with them.

First, you can have your Ghosts lock down each Tank, and then have your Pilots run to the beacons. This can be hard on your Ghosts, because they must take a hit before they can launch their Lockdown missile.

Second, if you have all three Medics travel together, you can blind each Tank with an Optical Flare, as two Medics heal the Medic taking the heat. Once the Siege Tanks are blinded, you're free and clear to get your Pilots to the beacons.

CAUTION

Watch out for the Spider Mine in Area 3. It can ruin your mission if it kills a Pilot.

Fig. 5-7. Use your Nukes whenever the enemy camp looks formidable.

At Area 3 you get your hands on four Nukes. You'll need them to get past heavy enemy defenses. The Science Vessel is the biggest impediment to Nuking enemy encampments. Have a Ghost lock down the Science Vessel and then bring in a Medic to render it blind with an Optical Flare. Then have another Ghost target a Nuke on the central unit in the enemy cluster. This will take out all but a few stragglers in the Bunkers. Do this three times in the three enemy camps: watching the Nukes go off is very satisfying. Move in with your Ghosts and Medics to clean up surviving enemies, or simply cloak your Ghosts and go after the helpless Marines and Firebats with stealth.

In Area 4, your two Tanks get locked down by a nearby enemy Ghost. Use your Medic's Restoration ability to "unlock" your Tanks so they can crush the Ghost. Move your Siege Tanks down the path a short distance, and then go into Siege Mode. This takes care of any advancing enemies and a nearby Bunker.

Several pesky Siege Tanks are positioned throughout this area, but your Ghosts have the answer. First, have your Ghosts lock down any nearby Science Vessels (or use an Optical Flare); then cloak your Ghosts and lock down and destroy each Siege Tank. Continue moving through this area until it's enemy-free. Move your Pilots to the beacons and get ready for some hot-and-heavy air-fighting.

Fig. 5-8. Lock down and destroy any Science Vessels so they can't spot for enemy Siege Tanks.

You get a group of Battlecruisers equal to the number you "liberated" from the Dominion in Area 5. A large group of enemy Battlecruisers approaches quickly from the north, so be ready for them. Your Battlecruisers are equipped with Yamato Cannons, so use them. As the enemy approaches, have two Battlecruisers target their Yamatos on *one* enemy Battlecruiser. Do this with all your units right off the bat, and you'll destroy half the enemy fleet before the action heats up. When you've exhausted your Yamatos, use your Battlecruisers en masse to attack one enemy at a time. This tactic ensures your troops a victory.

Fig. 5-9. Use your Yamato Cannons: that's what they're there for.

Resource Management

No resource management, as such, is involved in this scenario, but the number of units you have at each area is limited, so use them very carefully to get your Pilots to the Battlecruisers.

Mission 3: Ruins of Tarsonis

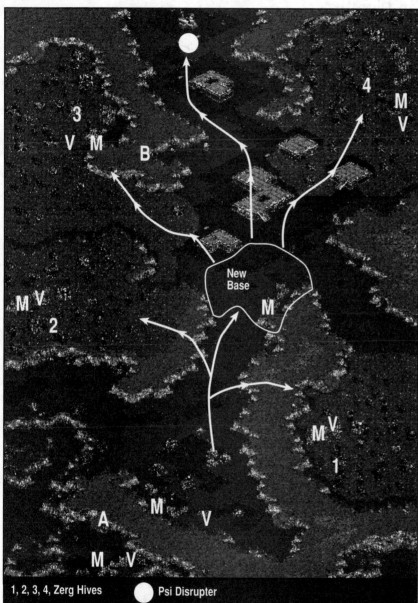

Fig. 5-10. Map of Terran Mission 3

The Psi Disrupter can lure the Zerg to its position, causing no end of chaos to them. Stukov has discovered the Psi Disrupter is on Tarsonis, where four Zerg broods guard it. It's impossible to make it to the Disrupter as long as the Zerg are in place, but Duran believes that destroying each Hive will render the corresponding Zerg harmless.

131

Mission Objectives

▼ Destroy the Zerg Hives to pacify the Zerg Broods.
▼ Take Duran to the Psi Disrupter after you destroy the Hives.

Special Units

Duran (Ghost)

Battle Strategy

This mission requires a lot of time and resources. There's just no easy way to claim victory: You must penetrate Zerg defenses and destroy each of the map's four Zerg Hives. The order is entirely up to you. The order set forth in the following paragraphs is just one way to attack the Zerg.

First, build some Bunkers and Missile Turrets on your base's perimeter. They'll provide the defense you need to survive the Zerg's initial attacks. After building your Bunkers and filling them with Marines, use a Dropship to transport an SCV to Area A, behind your base. This area has plenty of resources and you can exploit it quickly and in relative safety.

Once you've set up both bases, climb the tech tree as fast as you can. You must upgrade all your units' abilities before you can mount an attack on the Zerg.

Fig. 5-11. Build Bunkers and Missile Turrets to defend your primary base.

When you have Siege Tanks, Wraiths, and about 10 Marines (with Medics), load them into Dropships and deposit them on the ridge above Zerg Hive 1. The Siege Tanks will rain terror on Zerg defenses as your Marine–Medic group moves down the ramp to take out the Hive. Be ready with Wraith support, in case the Zerg respond with Guardians or Mutalisks.

TIP

When attacking a Zerg base, keep a Science Vessel handy to identify burrowed units. If you can spot them, your Siege Tanks can take them out in one shot.

Next, move your attack force to the middle of the map ("New Base" in figure 5-10) and build a Command Center. This area will undergo numerous attacks, so keep your Siege Tanks nearby and build Bunkers to defend the perimeter. You must build new units continually to manage the many Zerg attacks, but if you keep on top of it, with all three resource areas running, you won't have a problem.

Zerg Hive 2 is your next objective. Have a Dropship transport your units to the ridge where the Hive lies. A Science Vessel, three Siege Tanks, and a Marine–Medic group should be more than enough to take out this Hive. Hive 3 is difficult to approach over ground without taking a lot of casualties. I recommend dropping off Siege Tanks and Marine groups on the nearby ridge (Area B). After securing the ridge, you can take out the Hive with your Siege Tanks and never have to descend into the Zerg base. The Zerg will attempt to drop Ultralisks on the ridge using their Overminds: Keep your Marines ready to shoot the Overminds from the sky if they come near. Upgraded Goliaths also will do the trick.

Fig. 5-12. Once you've secured the ridge above Zerg Hive 3, bombard the Hive with your Siege Tanks.

You can approach Hive 4 over ground, but it's very well-defended. Use a slow-moving line of Siege Tanks and Marines to work your way toward the Hive, but be ready for attacks from Guardians, Queens, and Mutalisks. You've neutralized all the other Zerg hives, so pull all your forces together to wipe out this last Hive. Then move Duran to the Psi Disrupter to claim victory.

Resource Management

You must build up your base's defenses before you go looking for extra resources. Once your base is secure, move an SCV to Area A and build a Command Center right away. Build at least eight SCVs to harvest the minerals and Vespene there; you'll need all you can get in your battles against the Zerg.

The resource area in the center of the map ("New Base") isn't actually necessary, but you can use it. You can harvest resources from Zerg Broods that have lost their Hive, as well; they won't attack you at that point.

Resource concerns in this mission revolve around how fast you can harvest the resources—the faster the better.

Mission 4: Assault on Korhal

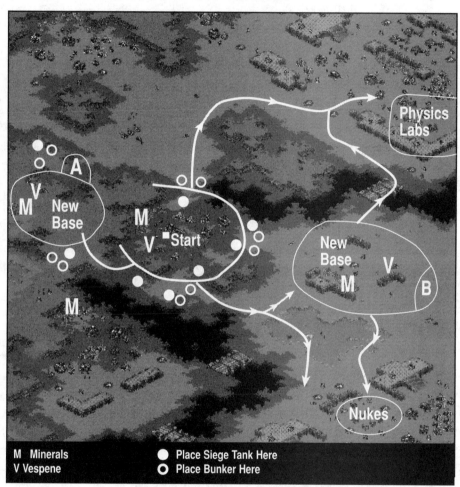

Fig. 5-13. Map of Terran Mission 4

Arcturas Mengsk has two main strategic settlements on Korhal. You can win this mission if you destroy them, but you have time to take out only one group of structures. You must eliminate either the Nuclear Silos or the Physics Labs: Your mission succeeds either way. But your decision will affect your next mission. There are two alternatives for Terran Level 5.

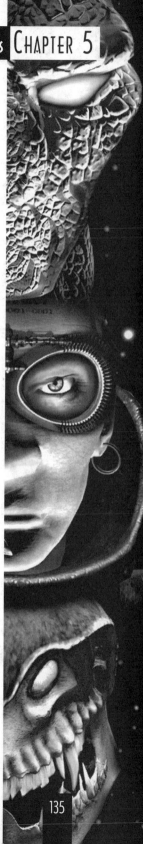

Mission Objectives

▼ Destroy either the enemy Physics Labs *or* the enemy Nuclear Silos.

Special Units

None

Battle Strategy

You must choose whether to destroy the enemy Physics Labs or wipe out their Nuclear Silos. You choice will determine whether you next end up in mission 5a or 5b. Both are great. I can say, however, that I've found it slightly easier to get at the Nukes in the map's lower-right corner.

TIP

Keep Medics around your Siege Tanks and Science Vessels in this mission. The enemy likes to perform Lockdowns on these, but your Medics can free a locked-down unit quickly using their Restoration ability.

First, build a new Command Center in Area A to double your resource income. Then lay down a defensive perimeter around your bases—Bunkers (filled with Marines), Siege Tanks, and Turrets (to spot cloaked units). You needn't build too many Turrets. Build Science Vessels, instead; they're mobile and have other abilities (such as Defensive Matrix and Irradiate).

Fig. 5-14. You'll undergo numerous enemy attacks, so keep your defenses frosty.

Climb the tech tree and upgrade your weapons and armor while you defend your two bases. After you reach these goals, send four to six Siege Tanks and a group of Marines and Medics to Area B. Have a Science Vessel accompany you in this attack, because plenty of cloakable enemy Ghosts are standing by. After securing this area, send in an SCV to build a new Command Center. Be sure to build a defense network around this area (Area B) as well, because the enemy will try hard to retake it.

TIP

Whenever you travel with Siege Tanks, Goliaths, or any air unit, be sure to keep an SCV around to repair damage. A simple SCV can save you a lot of resources.

From Area B, move to take out either the Nuclear Silos to the south or the Physics Labs to the north. Either way, use a balanced force of Siege Tanks and Marine–Medic groups to move up on enemy positions inch by inch. Keep a few Wraiths, a Science Vessel, and a pair of Ghosts with this attack group. The Wraiths can fend off air attacks, and the Science Vessel will let you see cloaked Ghosts or Wraiths. Use the Ghosts to target Nukes on problem areas of the enemy's defense network. If there's a pair of Bunkers you're finding hard to crack, nuke 'em to take them out, and then move your forces in to mop up.

Fig. 5-15. The going gets tough as you near your objective, but careful management of your Medics and SCVs can make for a quick victory.

The action is intense in both enemy camps, but advance your troops carefully and victory will be yours. Keep SCVs nearby to repair Siege Tanks and Medics nearby to heal Marines, and you should be able to work your way to the Nuclear Silos or Physics Labs.

Resource Management

If you can take Area A quickly, build a Command Center nearby, and defend it properly, you'll have no difficulty keeping yourself in resources. Don't skimp on SCVs. Use as many as you can to maximize your resource harvest. Use the raised ground near Area A to build the Supply Depots you'll need to support your growing army. This area provides natural protection from ground attack.

Area B offers plenty of resources, but once you've secured the area the enemy attacks it mercilessly, so weigh the pros and cons of waging a miniwar from that position. If you're adequately equipped, then Area B is very valuable, but if you must struggle constantly just to keep your structures intact, wait until you have the proper forces.

Mission 5A: Emperor's Fall (Ground Zero)

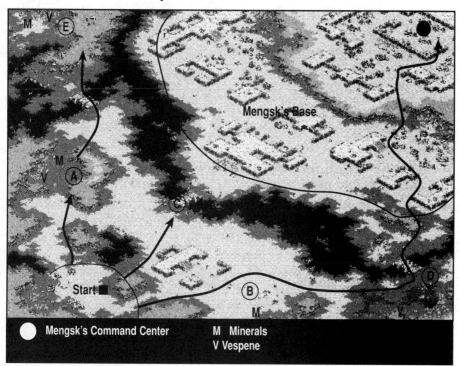

Fig. 5-16. Map of Terran Mission 5A

Dugalle advises you that, although Mengsk is unable to reinforce his armies, the Dominion still maintains a host of standing forces you'll have to deal with. Ever since you destroyed the Physics Labs in Mission 4, Mengsk's Battlecruiser fleet has been crippled. He is, however, expected to unleash his massive nuclear arsenal on your positions, so beware.

Mission Objectives

▼ Destroy Mengsk's Command Center.

Special Units

None

Battle Strategy

As this mission begins, Mengsk Ghosts knock the stuffing out of your forces with a series of particularly nasty nuclear strikes. This is expected; you'll just have to rebuild your forces after the barrage is done. If you're quick, you can save one or two structures by moving them to the side of the map as soon as you can. You certainly can fly your Barracks out of the blast radius if you move fast enough to get it off the ground.

After watching nukes toast your units, get back on the horse and rebuild your base. This usually starts with your Command Center: You'll probably need to repair it to get it out of the dangerous red zone that indicates severe damage. Your next priority is to build up your base until you can produce Science Vessels. Without them, enemy Ghosts will cloak and drop nukes out of detection range of your Missile Turrets until your base has been reduced to radioactive rubble. Once you have Science Vessels to spot them with, they become sitting ducks for your Marines, Vultures, or Tanks.

Fig. 5-17. Things look bad at the start, but you'll be able to rebuild in time to kick butt.

Take the resource nodes in areas A and B and build up appropriate defenses for these areas. Use Area B as an excuse to build a Command Center and Nuclear Silo. Build a force of Siege Tanks, Medics, a Science Vessel, at least one SCV, and a pair of Ghosts. Move this strike team up to Area C and let your Siege Tanks take out the Bunkers/Turrets there.

As soon as you start pummeling Area C, the enemy will send a bevy of Ghosts in to lock down your Siege Tanks, which is why you've brought the Medics along. Use your Medic's Restoration to "unlock" any affected Tanks and continue assaulting the enemy defenses. If you're having trouble taking the bridge, cloak one of your Ghosts and nuke the area. After securing the bridge, keep several Siege Tanks and a Science Vessel nearby to prevent the enemy from crossing it.

TIP

Constantly repair your Siege Tanks with your SCV and use your Medics not only to heal your Ghosts, but also to restore any Tanks that are crippled by Lockdown.

Fig. 5-18. A pair of Siege Tanks and a Science Vessel can provide a great defense for the bridge in Area C.

Move your attack force to Area D and build a base there, to acquire more resources. Move north up the map very slowly, advancing by using a combination of Nukes and Siege Tanks with Medic–SCV support. It's a tough haul, but you'll eventually make it up to Mengsk's Command Center. Whenever you come across a large group of structures, use your Nukes to take them out en masse. Remember, you need only take out Mengsk's Command Center to win—but you must hack through scores of enemy units to get there.

> **NOTE**
>
> Some players prefer to get to the Command Center using Battlecruisers moving up slowly with SCV support (much like Siege Tanks, but in the air). Although this method is riskier and more expensive, it's not without merit. Perhaps the best approach lies somewhere in between. What would it be like to have both Battlecruisers and Siege Tanks moving together?

Resource Management

You absolutely must capture resource Area A, but areas B, D, and E are optional, depending on your spending habits. Don't even *think* of mounting an attack on the enemy base until after you upgrade your weapons to their maximum levels, or Mengsk's elite troops will obliterate you. Blocking the bridge at Area C ultimately will save you plenty of resources, because then you won't constantly have to fend off broad attacks on your main bases. A few resources spent early on securing this location saves you grief later on.

Mission 5B: Emperor's Fall (Birds of War)

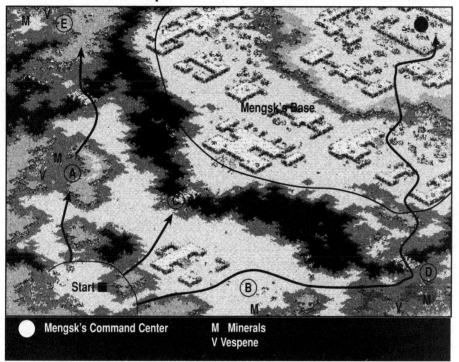

Fig. 5-19. Map of Terran Mission 5B

Dugalle advises you that, although Mengsk is unable to reinforce his armies, the Dominion still maintains a host of standing forces you'll have to deal with. Since you destroyed the Nuclear Silos in Mission 4, Mengsk's nuclear capabilities have been crippled. However, Mengsk is now expected to send his sizable Battlecruiser fleet to your positions, so beware.

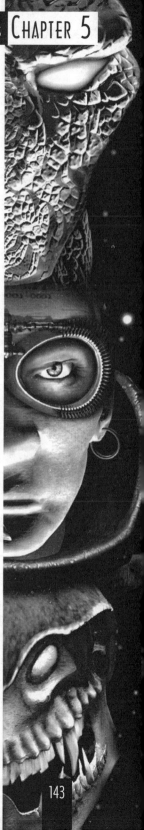

Mission Objectives

▼ Destroy Mengsk's Command Center.

Special Units

None

Battle Strategy

As this mission begins, a fleet of Battlecruisers annihilates all of your periph-eral outposts. As they head for your main base, you'll receive reinforcements consisting of upgraded Goliaths and Ghosts. When the Battlecruisers come into visual range, first use Lockdown on them and then unleash the Goliath's Hellfire rockets on the helpless targets. If you're quick, you can avoid having one or two of your structures destroyed by moving them to the side of the map as soon as possible. Your Barracks certainly can be moved out of the way if you move fast enough to get it off the ground.

After you repel the Battlecruiser attack and assess your damages, start rebuilding your base as quickly as possible. This usually starts with your Command Center, which will probably need repair to get out of the red zone. Your next priority is to build up your base to produce enough units to take Area A for its resources as well as to block the enemy's attacks from the bridges in areas C and E.

Fig. 5-20. The initial wave of Battlecruisers will hurt you, but the Goliaths you're left with will ease your pain.

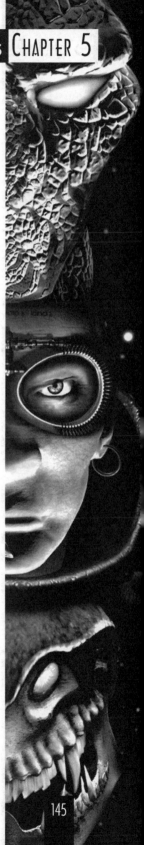

Take the resource nodes in areas A and B and build up appropriate defenses for these areas. Use Area B as a staging area for a Command Center with a Nuclear Silo attached. Build a force of Siege Tanks, Medics, a Science Vessel, at least one SCV, and a Ghost or two. Move this selection of units up to Area C and let your Siege Tanks take out the Bunkers/Turrets there.

As soon as you start pummeling Area C, the enemy will send a team of Ghosts in to use their Lockdown ability on your Siege Tanks. Unlock them using your Medic's Restoration ability. If you're having trouble taking the bridge area, cloak a Ghost and nuke the area to kingdom come. After securing the bridge, keep several Siege Tanks and a Science Vessel on alert to keep the enemy from crossing.

TIP

Continually repair your Siege Tanks with your SCV. Also, use your Medics to keep your Ghosts in excellent health and restore units stuck in Lockdown.

Move your attack force to Area D and build a base there if you need more resources. Move north up the map very slowly using a combination of Nukes and Siege Tanks with Medic–SCV support. Eventually you'll punch through to Mengsk's Command Center. Whenever you come across a large group of structures, use your Nukes to take them out en masse. Finally, remember that although you need only take out Mengsk's Command Center to complete the mission, you'll undoubtedly need to crush plenty of enemy units to get there.

Fig. 5-21. Move up the map with Siege Tanks and Ghosts with Nukes. If you don't rush it, you'll have great success, but don't forget to keep SCVs and Medics around for healing.

NOTE

Some players prefer to get to the Command Center using Battlecruisers moving up slowly with SCV support (much like Siege Tanks, but in the air). This method is both riskier and more expensive, although it's not without merit. Another idea that has merit is a combination of these two tactics—after all, who is going to argue with an armada of Battlecruisers *and* a battalion of Siege Tanks moving together?

Resource Management

You absolutely must capture resource Area A to ensure success, but areas B, D, and E are optional, depending on your spending habits. Don't even think of mounting an attack on the enemy base until after you upgrade your weapons to their maximum levels, or Mengsk's forces will make short work of you.

Blocking the bridge at Area C will save you lots of resources, because you won't constantly have to fend off attacks on your main bases. A few resources spent early on securing this strategically important location will save you plenty of grief later in the mission.

Mission 6: Emperor's Flight

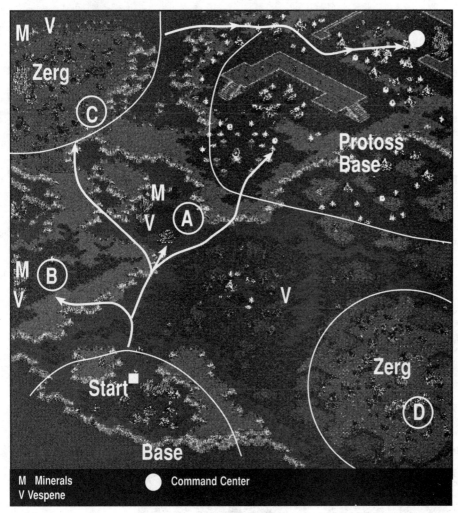

Fig. 5-22. Map of Terran Mission 6

The fugitives Mengsk and Raynor are on the Protoss homeworld of Aiur, hiding out in a Protoss base. Several Zerg Broods are mounting their units near the Protoss encampment, and this makes going after the fugitives a risky business. The admiral is sending down Valkyrie Frigates to back you up in your attempts to get Mengsk and Raynor.

Mission Objectives

▼ Destroy Raynor's Command Center.

Special Units

Raynor (in Dropship)

Battle Strategy

As this mission begins, you'll get to see the incredible power of a large group of Valkyrie Frigates as they unleash their attack on a wing of Zerg Mutalisks. After the Valkyries secure the area, shuttles drop a group of SCVs and Marines, and several structures will float in, as well. This will more or less give you an instant starting base. I suggest you begin fortifying it quickly, because the Zerg base in Area D will start launching attacks on your position soon.

Fig. 5-23. The Valkyries ride high in the beginning of this mission as they crush the Zerg air units.

After establishing your base, take the resource nodes in areas A and B. Neither is particularly difficult to capture, but once you've moved your troops in and set up a Command Center you can expect frequent attacks from both Zerg and Protoss encampments. Area A is an undefended resource node, but a small Protoss outpost lightly defends Area B.

Although the Zerg units "awaken" in a foul mood after you set up your base, not all the news is bad. The Zerg are angry *in general*, and will just as likely attack either the Protoss base *or* your base.

When you've established your bases, set up a defensive perimeter, and upgraded your units accordingly, make your move against the Zerg base in Area C. Send a group of Siege Tanks, one Science Vessel, and 10 Marines supported by two Medics to assault the base. (Lurkers are burrowed there, however, and without a Science Vessel to spot for you, they'll quickly turn you into carbon-based mush.) It's also a good idea to send your remaining Valkyries to take out the swarm of Mutalisk waiting in Area C. Don't rush your attack. Move up slowly, healing your units as you go. Hurrying your attack on Area C is a one-way ticket to defeat.

Fig. 5-24. Watch out for the Lurkers in and around the Zerg base in Area C.

By the time Area C is under your control, you should be close to the top of the tech tree. Thus, you'll be ready to mount an attack on the Protoss base. It won't be easy, and requires considerable resources and time. Consider mounting two attack waves, one from area C and one from Area A. The Area A wave should comprise the same units that attacked Area C (Siege Tanks, Marines, Medics, Science Vessel); the attack force from Area C could include Valkyries, Battlecruisers, and a Dropship or two full of Marines.

You may have to reinforce your attack several times, but once you gain a foothold in the outskirts of the Protoss base, you'll be able to work your way

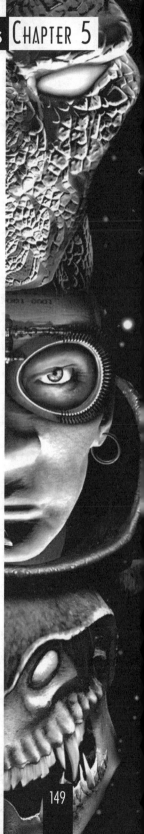

in toward the Command Center yard by yard. This requires lots of resources—and perhaps more than one attempt—so keep busy building reinforcements as you attack. Once you destroy the Command Center, you'll view about a minute of story line activity, and then you'll be awarded a victory.

Resource Management

This is a resource-intensive mission. Taking areas A and B is critical to have enough minerals and Vespene to upgrade your units sufficiently to battle either Zerg or Protoss. Don't worry about the resources in Area C, unless you're in a critical situation, where you're losing a battle of attrition. If this happens, fall back and harvest the resources in Area C to help with building a new attack force. Although Vespene shouldn't be scarce, there's an additional geyser located just southeast of Area A.

Mission 7: Patriot's Blood

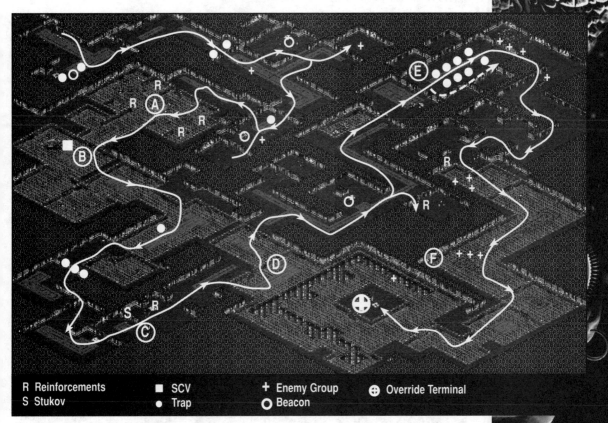

R Reinforcements	■ SCV	+ Enemy Group	⊕ Override Terminal
S Stukov	● Trap	○ Beacon	

Fig. 5-25. Map of Terran Mission 7

It appears Vice-Admiral Stukov did *not* destroy the Psi Disrupter, as we believed. Sensing treachery, Duran has convinced Admiral Dugalle to hunt down and destroy both Stukov and the Psi Disrupter. Although he can't believe his lifelong friend would turn against him, Dugalle sends Duran to the planet surface to deal with Stukov.

Mission Objectives

▼ Find and kill Vice-Admiral Stukov.
▼ Duran must survive.
▼ Get to Override Terminal before time expires.

Special Units

Duran (Ghost)
Stukov (Ghost)
Floor Traps

Battle Strategy

The key to this mission is to keep both Medics close to your Marines at all times. If you lose your Medics, you may lose the mission, so keep a close eye on them. This is an installation mission, so there's really only one way to play it. Your route is illustrated on the map in Figure 5-25. Although your path through the building is clear, there's plenty that you'll need to know about as you work your way through the mission.

Fig. 5-26. Keep your Medics close by at all times.

As you wind toward Area A, watch out for floor and wall traps, and remember to hop onto any beacons you come across. A UED Marine must activate beacons, so make sure you lead with them. When you reach Area A, you'll see a bunch of Goliaths that are ripe for the taking, as long as you can reach them before their Pilots can get to them and activate their defenses. If you get to them first, you'll have your own set of shiny new Goliaths to maneuver through the rest of this mission.

Even if you act quickly to get the Goliaths in Area A, you'll still end up fighting a Goliath or two in that area, so your newly acquired Goliaths probably will need repair. Don't worry, Area B has an SCV you can take with you on your travels.

Continue moving through the installation until you reach Area C, where Duran confronts Stukov. After this point, the Terran units in the installation will be your allies.

Fig. 5-27. Once Stukov is dead and Duran flees, the Terran units will become your allies.

As you move through Area D, you'll discover that not only do you have only a few precious minutes to throw the Override switch on the sabotaged reactor, but the base is overrun by Zerg. Keeping your Medics close to your Marines as you pass through the base is more important than ever. In Area E, you have a unique opportunity to shred a group of Zerg with the automatic floor guns mounted in the area. To lure the Zerglings into this area, move one of your soldiers to activate the door that's holding back the Zerglings, and then sit back and watch the carnage.

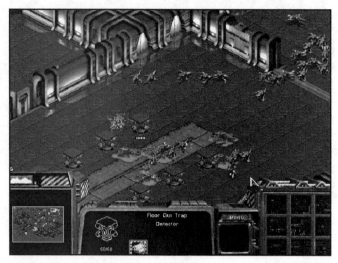

Fig. 5-28. It's nice to be able to relax and let the floor guns do the talking for a change.

Continue following the map path toward the Override Terminal. You'll encounter heavy Zerg resistance in and around Area F, but again, simply keep your Medics close to your Marines as the battles rage on and you'll be fine. When you get past Area F, you're almost home free. Simply get any unit onto the Override beacon to win the mission.

Resource Management

In this mission, resource management takes the form of using your Medics and SCV to optimize the health of all your units throughout the mission. It's even possible (although unlikely) to make it through the entire mission without losing one original unit—if you manage your healing and repair of units properly. Remember, don't rush in, and take the time to make sure your Medics are positioned well to administer battlefield care.

Mission 8: To Chain the Beast

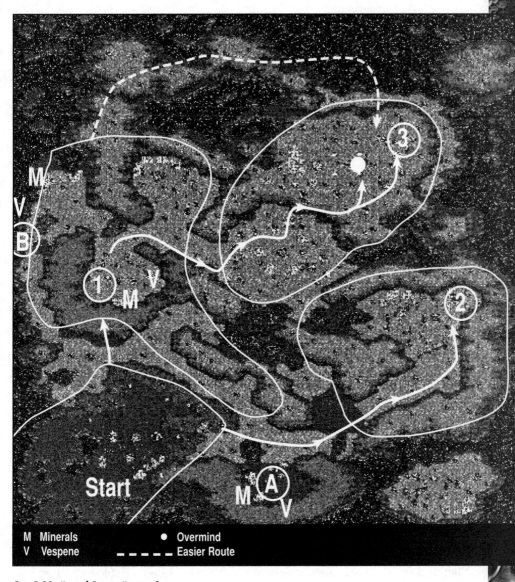

Fig. 5-29. Map of Terran Mission 8

The signal from the Psi Disrupter is hampering the Zerg's communications to each other and the swarms over Char have scattered in disarray. There are still plenty of Zerg defenses protecting the Overmind, however, including three Cerebrates with differing defensive abilities.

155

Mission Objectives

▼ Get a Medic to each of the beacons surrounding the Overmind.
▼ Kill Zerg Cerebrates to weaken the Overmind's defenses.

Special Units

Torrasque (Ultralisk Hero)
Kerrigan
Duran

Battle Strategy

This mission is a strange one in that many enemy defenses are indestructible until after you destroy one of the Zerg Cerebrates. This detail is something to worry about later, as you must begin this mission by building up your defenses *very* quickly. Put up a line of Bunkers, Turrets, and Siege Tanks around the perimeter of your base. A strong ground defense is important as you will have to face one Torrasque after another. What is a Torrasque, you ask? Torrasque is a very tough, fully upgraded Ultralisk hero killing machine that will continue to harass you until you've vanquished Cerebrate 2, so be sure you check that you have your Bunkers and Siege Tanks in order at your base. Also, you will need to build a Command Center in Area A to maximize your resource-gathering.

Develop your tech tree until you can build Battlecruisers and Valkyries. Then build four Battlecruisers and six Valkyries and get ready to rumble. Zerg Cerebrate 1 makes the red Sunken Colonies around your base invulnerable. You'll have to destroy that Cerebrate in order be able to attack and destroy the Sunken Colonies it controls. Move your Battlecruisers and Valkyries straight up to Cerebrate 1 and target it with four Yamato blasts, while the Frigates provide cover against any air attacks. Once the Yamatos have hit, finish off the Cerebrate quickly. As soon as it's been killed, Zerg forces there will fall dormant.

Fig. 5-30. Taking the first
Cerebrate from the
air is best.

After you kill Cerebrate 1, you'll face one Torrasque after another. Cerebrate 2 produces these Ultralisk Heroes, and they'll continue harassing you until you vanquish the Cerebrate. You're probably already amply set up to handle the Torrasque, but check to make sure you have your Bunkers and Siege Tanks in order at your base.

You'll take out the second Cerebrate the old-fashioned way. First, though, move your Battlecruisers along the route to Cerebrate 2 and take out all the Sunken Colonies along the way. After the Sunkens are gone, you're ready to launch a ground attack. Build at least four Siege Tanks, and three groups of 10 Marines and two Medics each; include a Science Vessel to spot Lurkers. As long as you keep your groups together (with their Medics), you can storm the Cerebrate en masse and kill it off. When it dies, the Zerg units around it will become dormant.

Fig. 5-31. A balanced
ground force like this one
makes destroying
Cerebrate 2 easier.

157

There are two ways to get to the third Cerebrate: you can pound right up through the middle of the base with Siege Tanks and support units, or you can use a group of eight Dropships to deposit a pair of Siege Tanks and a horde of Marines and Medics on the Cerebrate. It takes time to build up the forces, but less time and expense to mount the attack in the long run.

To make a landing successful, you must take three or more Battlecruisers up to Area B and use their Yamato Cannons to take out the first wave of Spore Colonies. Once those are destroyed, move your Dropships in quickly and let loose on the Cerebrate. Remember, you need to destroy the Cerebrate to silence the Zerg forces.

After you destroy Cerebrate 3, you need only place one Medic on each of the four beacons surrounding the Overmind.

You've won the mission and it's on to the Zerg campaign!

Resource Management

You definitely will need the resources in your home base, as well as in Area A. Depending on your tactical abilities, you may need Area B's resources, as well.

Basically, once a Cerebrate has been destroyed, you can take whatever you want from the area it controlled. If you need to gather resources from each Cerebrate's base after you kill each one, so be it. In the end there will be more than enough to support your attacks, but you must defend your bases sufficiently so you're not constantly rebuilding important structures.

The Zerg Missions

The Zerg is the last species you'll control in *Starcraft: Brood War*, and there are a pair of new units you must get used to—the Lurker and the Devourer. Now you'll deal directly with Kerrigan and the Zerg, as the plot of *Starcraft: Brood War* progresses toward its exciting conclusion.

Mission 1: Vile Disruption

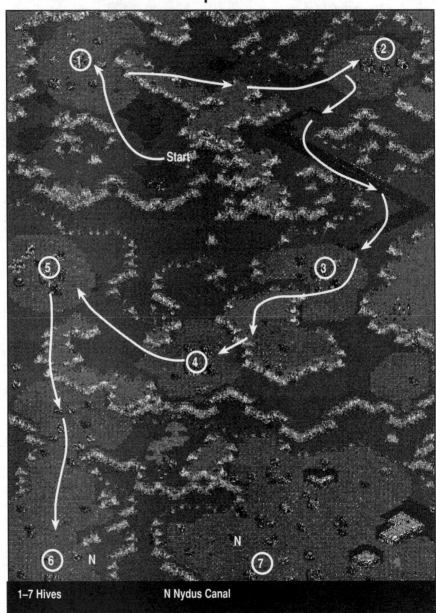

Start

| 1–7 Hives | N Nydus Canal |

06-Fig. 6-1. Map of Zerg Mission 1

Kerrigan is trying to recruit forces to defeat the UED and keep this sector from falling under its dominion, but the UED's Disrupter has reached Tarsonis and the Zerg forces are rampaging out of control, attacking their own Hives. You

must lead a small force of Zerg still under Kerrigan's leadership on a mission to save seven nearby Hives.

Mission Objectives

▼ Save all hives from destruction.

Special Units

None

Battle Strategy

When the mission starts, you'll spot a small Zerg force of six Hunter Killers and two Zerglings. Check the minimap for the locations of their seven Hives. The closest and easiest to reach is in the map's upper-left corner. Group your small band and send it north to save the first Hive.

As your forces approach the first Hive cluster, a band of eight Zerglings moves in and attacks the buildings around it. When your force comes into visual range, it falls under attack, as well. You should be able to defeat easily the eight renegade Zerglings assaulting this small base. When your forces move close enough to the Hive, a group of friendly Zerglings pops up from its burrows to assist you. This triggers another renegade force of six more Zerglings into the camp. You must also destroy these units before you can move to the next area.

Kerrigan reveals that you're unable to control the buildings you're rescuing, making reinforcements all but impossible. Thus, it's imperative that you use your forces wisely. You'll find additional friendly Zerg units at each Hive, but you don't have the limitless supply of units a Hatchery would provide.

You'll notice on the minimap that another Hive cluster has come under attack. This one lies in the map's upper-right corner. Send your Hunter Killers to the new location, but expect some resistance along the way. After you reach the second Hive cluster and defeat the attackers, move one of your units next to the Hive to gain control of it, and you'll acquire four Hydralisks to assist you.

A third Hive now becomes highlighted on the minimap. As you make your way toward this Hive, you'll be ambushed, so keep your forces together to fight off any assailants.

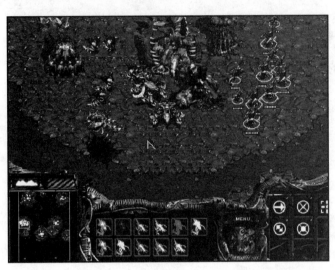

Fig. 6-02. Move quickly from one Hive to another to prevent the enemy from destroying them.

When you reach the third Hive, you'll gain control of a swarm of Scourges. These are useful immediately, because a Sunken Colony near the fourth Hive is under attack by three Zerg Guardians. If you don't defeat the Guardians before they destroy the Colony, they'll move on to the Hive cluster, so route your Scourges toward them right away. You have more than enough Scourge units to kill all three Guardians, so move any extras south to find two more Guardians waiting in ambush.

As your ground forces move toward the fourth Hive (in the center of the map), blocking terrain forces them to meander around. Along the way, they'll find a group of three Zerglings attacking a Spore Colony. Beware of this deception: the other two renegade Zerg Guardians lurk just west of the route that your ground forces will travel after defeating the three Zerglings. Attack each Guardian with all your units at once to kill it quickly before it can weaken your strike force.

TIP

Fight wisely, because your reinforcements are limited and you can't build new units in this mission.

The fun doesn't stop here, so be on alert as soon as you gain control of the fourth Hive. The Hive cluster falls under attack from north and west. Keep half your forces on those two sides of the camp. A Sunken Colony will assist you, so let the enemy attackers come into range of the cluster before defending against them. If you keep your six Hunter Killers on the west side of the camp and let them contend with the attackers there, the Hydralisks you gain at this fourth camp will supplement your remaining Hydralisks and Zerglings. Station these to the north of the camp. Be wary of attackers coming in waves: don't let your guard down until the next Hive is highlighted.

Fig. 6-03. The fifth Hive cluster will be under heavy attack; you'll have to hurry to save it.

The fifth Hive is in the middle of the left side of the map. Move your forces toward it when you get the message that it's under attack. You'll find a renegade force of Hydralisks and Zerglings there that you can defeat after a short battle. As soon as you control the Hive, two Ultralisks will head up from the south and attack this camp. You gain control of four Queens, as well, but don't use their special powers yet.

When this fifth Hive cluster is safe, move your forces south toward a group of Ultralisks attacking a small outpost of Zerg buildings. Use the Queens' Spawn Broodling ability to wipe out these mammoth beasts. Another Ultralisk may be revealed to the east, battling four newly acquired Hydralisks. You should have one Queen left with enough energy to destroy the Ultralisk.

The sixth Hive cluster lies in the map's lower-left corner. It's under attack by eight Mutalisks. Move your forces there to engage the renegades and save the Hive.

Fig. 6-04. This Nydus Canal is your transport to the seventh Hive.

At the sixth Hive cluster, locate the Nydus Canal as quickly as possible. It lies just north and east of the Hive, and is the only way to get your units into the area around the seventh Hive. When you get the message that the seventh Hive is under attack, you'll see on the minimap that quite a large contingent of renegade Zerg units causing wanton destruction. Your best hope is to reach the final Hive structure, because controlling it will give you a host of new units with which to fight. You'll probably find this new host very useful, as countless more renegades pop up for the final battle. If you reach the Hive quickly enough, the battle will be long but the outcome will be favorable.

Resource Management

There are no resources to collect or harvest in this mission. There are no buildings to control, and so no upgrades to research or technology paths to complete. Using your units effectively is the only thing you need to worry about during this mission.

Mission 2: Reign of Fire

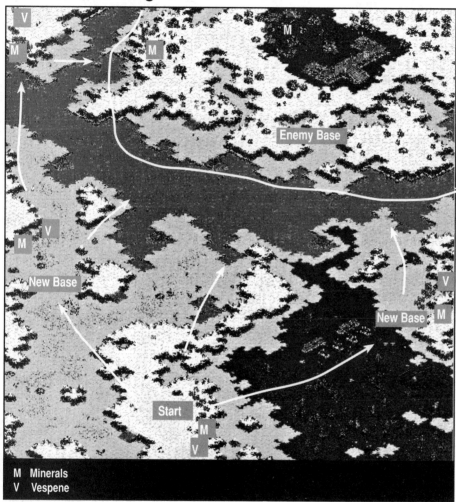

Fig. 6-5. Map of Zerg Mission 2

Kerrigan seeks to gain control of all the Zerg Broods. She's enlisted the aid of Jim Raynor and Arcturus Mengsk, who'll assist you in destroying the power generator for the Psi Disrupter. Mengsk will also provide a Psi Emitter to capture and control enough ungoverned Zerg units to build an attack force. You must capture the wandering Zerg, build up a sizeable offensive force, and find (and destroy) the Psi Disrupter.

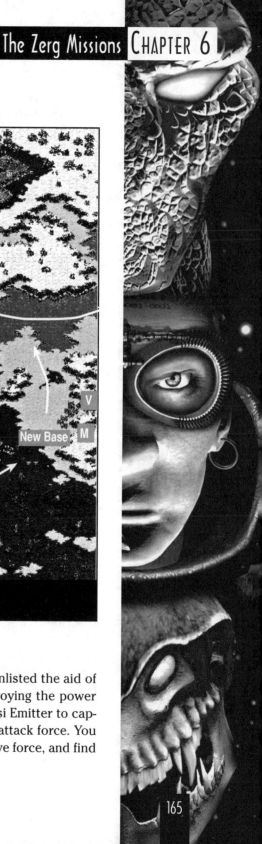

Mission Objectives

▼ Destroy the Psi Disrupter.

Special Units

Terran SCV with Psi Emitter, used to capture control of Zerg units

Battle Strategy

This mission starts with a few minutes of scripted action as Raynor's Raiders destroy the generator that powers the Psi Disrupter.

Once you gain control of the Terran SCV with the Psi Emitter, you can wander around and find Zerg units to control. You'll find two Zerg Drones immediately left of the SCV. Touch them with the Psi Emitter and build a Zerg Hatchery near the mineral fields and Vespene Geyser in the area. You'll have to build Overlords before you can create more than one additional Drone. Be sure to concentrate on harvesting crystal and gas for the first few minutes of the game.

Another resource patch lies along the left side of the map, in the middle. You'll encounter Terran Marines, Firebats, and a few Medics, so you must capture a force of Zerg units before taking this area.

There are eight Zerglings you can convert with the Psi Emitter in the area around your camp. There are three Hunter Killers at the bottom of the ramp leading down from your base. Use these nine units to work your way along the valley leading north to the next mineral patch. You'll find some Devouring Ones (hero-level Zerglings) by the time you finally reach the minerals. The resistance you encounter mainly comprises Terran Marines in Bunkers backed up by a Siege Tank. If you send the Zerglings straight for the Tank and let the Hydralisks cut away at the Bunkers, you should minimize your losses. If you head east from the mineral fields, you'll find the awesome Ultralisk, Torrasque.

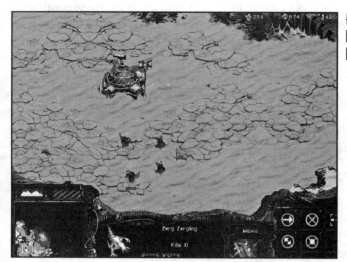

Fig. 6-06. This odd-looking building marks the valley branch you must defend.

The valley leading away from your base branches right, where you'll find another Terran Bunker and Siege Tank. The same strategy you used earlier will be as effective here, or you can send in Torrasque and watch him rip through the Terran defenses, much like he did to *you* in Terran Mission 8. Farther beyond is a group of three more Hunter Killers. These are the last of the native Zerg units you'll find. At this point, the Terran SCV you've been controlling finally loses his nerve and calls for dust-off. You must build up forces on your own from now on.

Keep forces stationed where the valley branches, because a group of Terrans will attempt to infiltrate your base and make trouble. They could come down either branch. Don't exploit the second mineral patch until you have enough forces to secure both branches of the valley.

While you explore and secure the valley, expand your base. Build Spore Colonies to defend against air attacks, because your forces guarding the valley will handle most ground attacks. A small force of Terran Wraiths visits your base after awhile, so the Spore Colonies are critical. Build the Spawning Pool, Evolution Chamber, and Hydralisk Den as soon as you can; this will let you increase your ground troops' effectiveness. When these buildings are ready, you can evolve the Burrowing ability and change your Hatchery into a Hive.

After securing the valleys and establishing production at the second mineral patch, concentrate on building up your forces to attack the Psi Disrupter. Plan to attack with at least four full groups of units, mixing Zerglings and Hydralisks to make sure you can counter any air threat. You'll have to send more units to resupply your attack force during the battle, but I recommend a minimum of four groups of attackers before the first assault.

Fig. 6-07. Attack the Psi Disrupter with a balanced force of Hydralisks and Zerglings.

The Terran base lies in the upper-right corner of the map. Your first group of attackers should concentrate on taking out Terran Siege Tanks and Bunkers. Let subsequent waves worry about the other buildings, because if you don't neutralize the Siege Tanks, your forces will diminish too rapidly. A small group of Mutalisks is helpful here, if you can sneak them to the upper-left corner of the map. Bring them in behind the main Terran camp. There they can divert attention from your main attack force. Don't try to fly the Mutalisks straight into the Terran base; it's heavily guarded by Missile Turrets.

You'll find the Psi Disrupter in an alcove in the upper-right corner of the map, about a quarter of the way in from the right edge. You don't need to destroy all the Terran buildings, because once the Disrupter is gone, your mission is complete. You'll have less trouble with the Disrupter, however, if you destroy the bulk of the Terran base first.

Resource Management

A good supply of minerals and Vespene Gas is essential. You should have 10 to 12 Drones harvesting minerals at each base. Two or three Drones per Refinery collecting gas should be sufficient.

When you start to build up your small force of Mutalisks, you may run short of Vespene, but don't concentrate your forces on Mutalisks, because the Terrans have an effective Missile Turret array waiting for them. You may decide to establish a third base to collect more resources, but it's not necessary; the mission is well within your reach with the resources available from the two outposts.

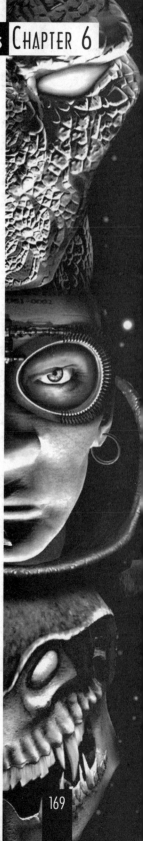

Mission 3: The Kel-Morian Combine

Fig. 6-8. Map of Zerg Mission 3

Although Fenix and Raynor sense that Kerrigan can't be trusted, the UED are a larger threat, so working with Kerrigan becomes the lesser of two evils. The Kel-Morian Combine is one of the system's largest resource nodes, and, if you can help Kerrigan defeat enemy forces and grab control of the resources, she'll have what she needs to take out the UED.

Mission Objectives

▼ Build up 10,000 mineral resources.
▼ Infest the Terran Command Centers.
▼ Fenix must survive.

Special Units

Fenix, a Protoss Dragoon

Battle Strategy

You begin in the lower-left corner of the map with a large assortment of Zerg units and Fenix, a Protoss Dragoon. Fenix must survive the mission, so protect him at all costs. Your other warrior units are Zerglings, Hydralisks, a Queen, and two Ultralisks. You also have eight Drones and four Overlords with which to start your first base.

Your first base isn't free, however. You must attack a small Terran base northeast of your starting position and destroy all enemy buildings there to set up your Hatchery and begin harvesting resources. A small detachment of Marines and Goliaths, and one Bunker containing four Marines, protect the Terran Base. Your force of Zerglings and Hydralisks can handle the Marines easily, but you should send your Ultralisks to destroy the enemy Bunker. When all opposition is eliminated from this area, you can build your base.

Fig. 6-09. Ultralisks are good units to take on Bunkers with.

The only land route into this first area is via Area A, in the northeast. Marshal your troops there to protect against curious Terran units that attack regularly. The Terrans also will use Dropships to land Marines behind you, so keep some Zerglings and Hydralisks at the back of your base. Building an array of Spore Colonies is a good idea, and you may as well keep Fenix back there, too, because he can defend against Dropships without getting into trouble.

The rest of the map is heavily populated with Terran forces. There are five main enemy camps, though the Terrans also have stationed sentries at key points. There are numerous Terran Missile Turrets, so using air units on this map requires diligence. The map layout is a series of valleys connecting the Terran camps, restricting your overland routes to narrow corridors and well-defended choke points. In other words, they know you're coming, and they have you covered—in the air and on the ground!

Take time to build up your first base before attacking any of the other Terrans. You'll have enough minerals and Vespene Gas at your first camp to build all the base structures available to you. Upgrading all your warrior units is also a good idea. The Terran camps are all of about equal strength, so there's no best one to attack first. You must hit them hard right from the start.

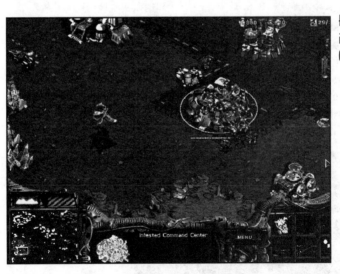

Fig. 6-10. Your goal is to infest as many Command Centers as possible.

Your task in this mission is to infest the Terran Command Centers. To wear the Command Center down enough for your Queen to infest it, you must defeat the forces protecting it. Keep an eye on your units so they don't inadvertently destroy the Command Center before the Queen is finished with it.

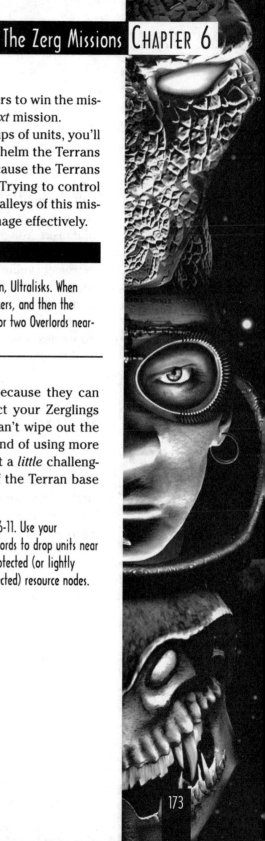

Although you don't *need* to infest any of the Command Centers to win the mission, the more you capture, the better off you'll be in the *next* mission.

If you attack each Terran base with three or four full groups of units, you'll make good progress. Four groups won't be enough to overwhelm the Terrans in one wave, so you'll have to rebuild more groups. But because the Terrans won't replace their buildings, you'll not lose much ground. Trying to control more than four groups of units is too difficult in the narrow valleys of this mission, so concentrate on directing the units that you can manage effectively.

TIP

Each of your groups should include Zerglings, Hydralisks, and, when you have them, Ultralisks. When attacking a Terran camp, send your units after the Siege Tanks first, then the Bunkers, and then the enemy units. The Terrans will use cloaked Wraiths and Vulture Mines, so keep one or two Overlords nearby to spot these units for your warriors.

The Zerglings are very effective against Siege Tanks because they can attack from inside the Tank's minimum attack range. Direct your Zerglings against the Tanks in a group of at least three so the Tank can't wipe out the entire group before it gets in close. The Terrans are quite fond of using more than one Siege Tank at a time (after all, they want to make it a *little* challenging for you) so watch carefully as your units reveal more of the Terran base they're attacking.

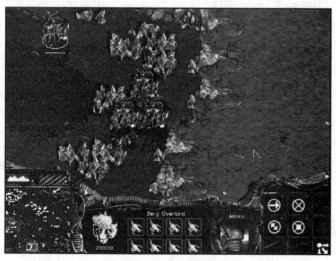

Fig. 6-11. Use your Overlords to drop units near unprotected (or lightly protected) resource nodes.

You'll find some resource patches on the plateaus above the valleys, but Terrans protect almost all of them. In some cases you can use your Overlords to lift units onto the plateau, out of the range of the Terran defenses, and then attack. Some Terrans are in range of your Hydralisks from the valleys below. Or you can choose to destroy some Terran Missile Turrets the hard way—with air units. After you establish at least two camps and have enough resources, build a Spire, and then a Greater Spire, and a small group of Mutalisks. You then can morph the Mutalisks into Guardians and take out the Missile Turrets from beyond their maximum range. The Guardians are extremely vulnerable to other, faster, enemy units, however. Their cost makes them too valuable to lose, so they are unsuitable for attacking the main Terran bases.

It's not necessary to destroy every Terran structure. Once you've infested or destroyed all five Terran Command Centers on the map or collected 10,000 minerals, you win the mission.

Resource Management

The resources in the first area are enough to build up a good base, but you must expand to reach your goals. If you take out one Terran base at a time and start exploiting its mineral patch, you'll stay well stocked.

Don't ignore the minerals on the plateaus. They make a great supplement to your war effort. You must have 10,000 minerals to complete the mission, unless you intend to infest all five Command Centers.

Mission 4: The Liberation of Korhal

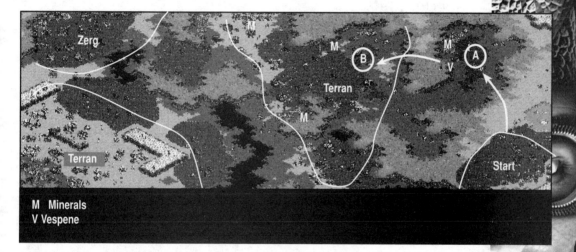

Fig. 6-12. Map of Zerg Mission 4

Now that the resources you've gathered are stored and everyone's ready, the time has come to attack the heavily defended UED base on Korhal, ostensibly to return the planet to Arcturas Mengsk. Kerrigan, however, might have other ideas …

Mission Objectives

▼ Destroy all enemy bases.

Special Units

None

Battle Strategy

You begin in the lower-right corner of a short, wide map. Three of the Terran Command Centers you infested in the previous mission are at your disposal, along with four Hatcheries and some Drones. You must build this base up quickly to fend off regular attacks from your enemies—in this case, Terrans and Zerg. Expect to see an enemy Zerg Ultralisk within a few minutes.

The rest of the map can access your first base in three places—passages to the north, nearby to the northwest, and west. Keep sentry units on the northwest side of your camp, because this is the most common route for enemy attacks.

You start with the 10,000 minerals you gathered in the previous mission, but there's a desperate shortage of Vespene Gas on this map. You have one Vespene Geyser at your base, but only one won't allow you to harvest fast enough for your needs. A second resource patch, including a geyser, lies north of your position, at Area A (northeast map area). It's occupied by a small group of Terrans in three Bunkers and three Missile Turrets. This should be your first conquest.

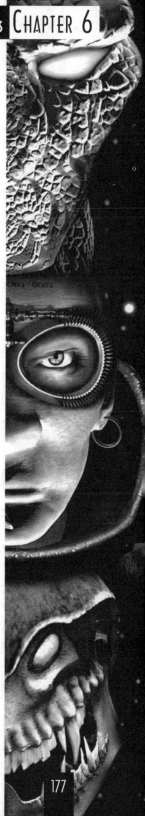

Fig. 6-13. Zerglings will be your best units right off the bat, mostly because they don't require Vespene.

You have limited Vespene Gas with which to build units, so produce mainly Zerglings for the first attack. Two or three full groups should let you take over the new resource node at Area A. Build a Hatchery, and then fortify this location with Sunken Colonies and Spore Colonies. When you have about five of each colony, build a second Hatchery. You'll win this mission through sheer numbers, so you must be able to create a lot of units.

The Terrans and enemy Zerg forces are intermixed through most of the map. Your forces must include Hydralisks to counter air threats and Overlords to spot hidden units like Lurkers and Wraiths. After you've established and fortified your first two camps, spend some time building structures to upgrade your warriors. Focus on Zerglings and Hydralisks; one or two groups of Guardians will come in very handy, however, so build a Greater Spire and upgrade air attacks.

You'll be attacked by Guardians escorted by an enemy Overlord, and separately by Marines and Siege Tanks. A few Spore Colonies and Sunken Colonies at each camp should reinforce the Hydralisks and Zerglings you're building up.

When you've upgraded your units and are ready to attack, follow the northern passage to the first ramp into Area B (central map area). You must clear a number of widely scattered Terran and enemy Zerg structures and units in this area. Expect to face Marines, Firebats, and Goliaths. Guardians are great, if you have them, for wiping out the enemy Sunken Colonies. Watch out for Missile Turrets.

A small enemy base lies south of Area B, on the edge of the map. It's very well fortified with Missile Turrets and Sunken Colonies. Ignore it until you have a group of Guardians with which to attack. Remember to send along an Overlord to watch for cloaked Wraiths and Lurkers, and Hydralisks to deal with angry Marines.

In the northwest corner of Area B lies one of the main Terran camps. After you wipe it clean of enemy units and buildings, you should establish your own base there. Although you control more than half the map now, the mission isn't yet half over. Build two Hatcheries at your third camp to help produce units faster.

There's only one ground route, to the west, for finding the next enemy camp. It's the main Zerg camp, and it, too, is defended well by Sunken Colonies and Lurkers. You'll run into some sentries along the way, but you'll know you've found the Zerg base when you reach the map's northwest corner.

Fig. 6-14. Set a rally point outside the Zerg base so your units will show up automatically.

If you set the rally point for your Hatcheries/Hives to a position near the enemy Zerg camp in the northwest corner, you can maintain a steady supply of units. Continue the strategy of producing large numbers of cheap units, such as Zerglings and Hydralisks. By the time you're ready to attack the Zerg base, you should have at least six Hatcheries and Hives. When you have at least five or six full groups of units, you can begin your assault.

You won't be able to completely destroy every unit in the Zerg main camp without using Mutalisks, because some of the enemy Zerg air units will hide in the extreme corner of the map, where your ground units can't reach them.

A group of Mutalisks can clean up the remnants of the Zerg base, and then morph into Guardians for the attack on the remaining Terran camp. Be sure to keep a few Mutalisks around to support your Guardians against Valkyries, Wraiths, and Scourges.

The last camp lies in the southwest corner of the map, and is accessible only to land units, through the area where the enemy Zerg main base was. The Terrans have strategically located a Siege Tank on a plateau your land units can't climb. Guardians are the best units to use to take out the Siege Tank, but protect them with Mutalisks, Hydralisks, and Overlords, because the Terrans will send Wraiths and everything else they have left.

CAUTION

There are a number of enemy Zerg Scourge units mingling with the Terrans in their camp, so keep an eye on your air units even after the Terrans seem worn down.

You must create wave after wave of units to wear down Terran defenses, so organize your rally points so new units are delivered near the battle. This minimizes the time you spend organizing and routing your units. You should have a lot of practice grouping units by now, and attacking with five or six groups at once is necessary in this battle. When you've eliminated all enemy structures, you win.

Depending on how you chose to approach the previous mission, you may have one or more infested Command Centers. Infested Marines are exceptionally effective against bunker and Turret emplacements, and since you went to all the trouble of getting them in the first place, you might as well use them!

Resource Management

The critical issue in this mission is Vespene Gas. You must secure a supply from at least two, preferably more, sources at the same time. The resource node to the north of your first camp is therefore critical to victory: conquer it quickly. You need upgrade only one of your Hatcheries to a Lair, and then a Hive. Upgrading the others is a waste of resources.

You'll be tempted to produce heavy units such as Ultralisks, but it's more cost effective to build cheap units. A small number of Mutalisks you can morph into Guardians will serve you well, however.

Mission 5: True Colors

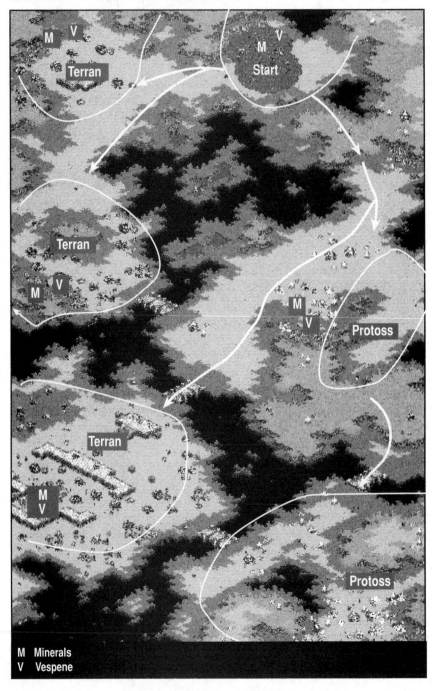

M Minerals
V Vespene

Fig. 6-15. Map of Zerg Mission 5

Now that the UED's power base on Korhal is broken, only its forces on Char pose any significant threat to Kerrigan. The Queen of Blades has decided to destroy General Duke and Fenix to eliminate the threat their tactical abilities pose to her plans. Duran will launch an attack on the base housing Duke and Fenix, with instructions to slaughter all enemies in Kerrigan's name.

Mission Objectives

▼ Destroy the enemy bases.
▼ Kill Duke.
▼ Kill Fenix.

Special Units

Duke
Fenix

Battle Strategy

This mission opens with a few seconds of scripted action, as three Zerg Lurkers move in on a group of Terran and Protoss units loitering in a small valley. The Lurkers burrow into the soil and rip up the unsuspecting group. They then unborrow and lead you back to your base. All enemy structures are visible from the start of this mission.

Once you gain control of your base, you have six minutes during which the Terrans and Protoss produce no new units. Use this time to destroy as much of the enemy forces as you can. The Terrans are located all along the west side of the map, and the Protoss are on the east. Because the Terrans are slightly closer to you, they're the best to attack. Send your Hydralisks and Zerglings to the first Terran camp in the northwest corner and wipe out everything.

During the game's opening minutes, you should produce only Zerglings and Hydralisks. Set your existing Drones to collect minerals, but don't bother creating new Drones or structures: it's critical to wipe out as much of the Terran bases as you can.

When you launch your attack on the second Terran base, concentrate on structures used to create higher-level Terran units, such as the Factory and Barracks. If you destroy these buildings before time runs out, the Terrans can't produce those units to attack you. Also, make sure you take out the Bunkers and any units trying to defend the base.

181

Fig. 6-16. The clock is running. Take out the Terran bases quickly, if you can.

In the six minutes at the beginning of this mission, you should be able to do enough damage to disable the first two Terran camps completely. After the counter runs out, concentrate on fortifying the areas you captured, including your original base. The Protoss will respond first, because you didn't diminish their ability to make war, so be prepared. Create at least six Sunken Colonies around your starting location. When you have enough Sunken Colonies, create an equal number of Spore Colonies. Station several Hydralisks near your encampment, as well. The forces you used to destroy the Terran bases should continue cleaning up the Terran structures.

Notice that the two areas you captured from the Terran army are accessible from only one direction—a bridge at the south end of the area. Position your warriors near the entrance to this bridge so you can contain any intruders. The Protoss will attack your main camp from the south and east. Expect most of the action to come from the south. The most difficult part of this mission is surviving the counterstrikes that occur almost immediately after the six-minute countdown.

After you secure your section of the map, build four more Hatcheries near the resource patches you acquired. Like all Zerg missions, this one will depend on how fast you can create units. Also, build the structures you need to upgrade your Zerglings and Hydralisks. And don't forget to build Spore Colonies near your expansion bases to counter air threats: the Terrans and the Protoss will use the skies against you if you let them.

When you've upgraded your units and built a sizable attack force, concentrate on wiping out the first two Protoss outposts—the ones located in the northeast and east parts of the map. The Protoss use Dark Templars,

Arbiters, and Observers quite often in this battle, so keep a few Overlords around to spot hidden units. Your attack groups should comprise a mix of Zerglings and Hydralisks. You needn't create any more expensive units at this point, because the first two Protoss camps are relatively easy to destroy. By producing units continuously from all six Hatcheries/Hives, you can overwhelm the Protoss defenders.

Fig. 6-17. Use mass production from multiple Hatcheries to overwhelm the Protoss.

If you begin your attack on the Protoss from the north and move southward, eventually you'll be in the right place to continue your attack on the main bases in the south. Keep a garrison at the bridge entrance near the second Terran camp you destroyed, but move all your attackers north and let them move south through the Protoss outposts.

Concentrate your attackers on the Protoss Photon Cannons and Dragoons. These threaten your escorting Overlords: Destroy them first. Reavers also are very destructive and should be a priority. You can ignore Pylons until you've destroyed all other structures in the area.

After destroying the first two Protoss outposts, you'll discover a bridge leading to each remaining base. A bridge connects the two camps, as well, so as you attack one, locate this connecting bridge and block it with units so you don't get caught from behind.

It doesn't matter which enemy base you attack first at this point. The main bases are quite rigorously defended, so you may want to include heavy units such as Guardians and Ultralisks in your attack groups. Because these units are very expensive, you may find producing them difficult to support for long. Keep careful watch over them, and don't let your best units be destroyed for

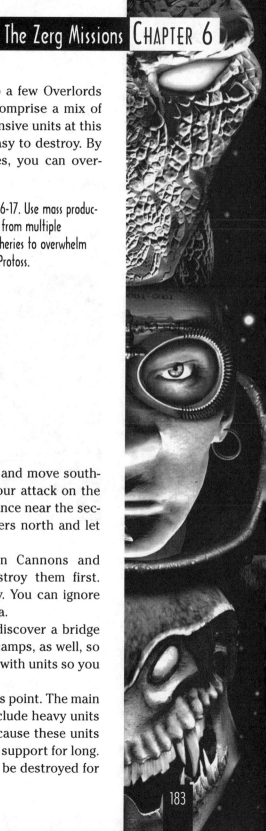

nothing; if Ultralisks are under attack by Terran Battlecruisers, they can't fight back, so let them retreat until your Hydralisks can intervene.

In the main Terran base, you'll find Battlecruisers, Wraiths, Siege Tanks, and all the other regular Terran units. A couple of Siege Tanks strategically perch atop a nasty plateau you can't ascend, so if you have Guardians available, you may find them useful when you spot these Tanks. Sending in a full group of Hydralisks is a great way to destroy a Battlecruiser. The Hydralisks aren't expensive to produce and they make short work of the Terran air unit. Keep your Zerglings and Ultralisks busy on Siege Tanks and Missile Turrets, while the Hydralisks go after these and other air units.

Fig. 6-18. Hydralisks are good for dealing with Battlecruisers.

In the Protoss camp you'll find a seemingly limitless supply of Reavers and Carriers. The Reavers take up a position on their side of the bridge and make it difficult for you to get enough units across to do any real damage. To counter this tactic, use air units such as Mutalisks or Guardians: Reavers can't attack air units. But the Reavers are seldom alone, and the other Protoss warriors can cause a lot of trouble for a Guardian, who *also* can't attack air units.

Another way to defeat the Reavers is to make them waste their shots on your Zerglings. If you build up enough Zerglings, they can rush the bridge nonstop until the Reaver is destroyed; then you can move other unit types into the Protoss camp and do some real damage.

TIP

The Protoss Carriers are deceptively easy to destroy. Using a full group of Hydralisks, attack the Carrier and ignore the ships it sends out. When the Carrier is gone, the ships will self-destruct.

Arbiters are in abundance in the final Protoss camp, and they're a nuisance. You must keep moving Overlords into the battle so you can see what the Arbiters are hiding, and when you try to attack an Arbiter it will flee to higher terrain or behind its own lines. Mutalisks or Scourges become very effective weapons against the Arbiters, but they're vulnerable on their own. The trick to defeating the Protoss main camp is to coordinate all your units so no single type of unit attacks the camp alone.

When you find Fenix, he'll speak to Kerrigan briefly, and then attack you. You must destroy Fenix to win the mission.

When all enemy structures are destroyed, and Duke and Fenix are dead, you win the mission.

Resource Management

You must control at least three mineral patches, as well as three Vespene Geysers, and exploit them concurrently. You'll need at least six Hatchery/Hive structures to produce units, and because you'll produce continuously, arrange the rally points so you're not spending time routing your warriors to the battle. This mission, like every classic battle, is a challenge in time and resource management. You must check on your Hatcheries to make sure you're creating units quickly and efficiently, check on your resources to make sure you're not running out, and check on your warriors to make sure they're fighting well. You'll almost certainly expend all the resources at two or three of your bases, so locate and establish footholds at new resource nodes as you expand your domain.

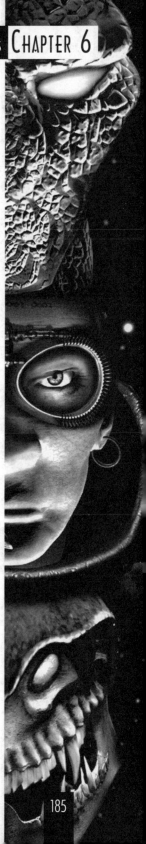

Mission 6: Fury of the Swarm

Fig. 6-19. Map of Zerg Mission 6

Hundreds of renegade Zerg have landed on Tarsonis, and this can only result from the UED using its Psi Disrupter to pit their Zerg against those controlled by Kerrigan. Kerrigan is ready for the challenge, however, and her minions will fight to the death if necessary.

Mission Objectives

▼ Destroy the renegade Zerg. After a few minutes, your mission objective changes:
destroy the UED Scientists at the Terran base.

Special Units

Terran Scientists

Battle Strategy

You begin this mission on an island in the middle of a ring of islands. Although
you're inaccessible to land units, the islands around you are connected,
except between the ring's north and south half. You have four outposts located on the ring islands, but they fall under attack immediately. Don't bother trying to save the outlying bases on the ring islands; instead concentrate on
building your central base.

You'll need to defend your central island from air assaults, so you'll need
Spore Colonies. Because your space is limited, use Hydralisks and Zerglings
for ground defense instead of building Sunken Colonies. You must build a
Spawning Pool and Hydralisk Den because the ones in your ring camps will be
destroyed. Keep ground defenses stationed on your central island throughout
this mission to fend off transported enemy units.

Fig. 6-20. Let your outlying
bases fall early and
concentrate on defending
your main base.

187

The enemy attackers that eliminate your camps will disperse when their job is done, leaving several prime locations for setting up expansion bases. Of course, you'll have to research Ventral Sacs for the Overlords before you can lift your units to the new resource patches. Because enemy Zerg Hatcheries already are being developed at the vacated resource nodes, send Hydralisks and Zerglings along with your Drones to clean up the enemy structure in each area. A few Lurkers await you on these islands, as well, so use Overlords to spot them.

You can expand to the islands either north or south of your central base. It's unnecessary to expand in both directions; in fact, it's difficult to do so, because enemy Zerg forces will keep you busy enough trying to establish control over just one half of the ring. Send air units to attack the half you don't conquer to minimize attacks from this direction.

Your three enemies' main encampments lies along the west edge of the map. There's only one land route in the north and one in the south from which your expansion bases are accessible, so station your warriors at the choke points leading west.

Build two Hatcheries at each of the two resource nodes you find. Air units are very useful on this map, so build the structures you need to develop Mutalisks and Guardians. Spend equal resources building and upgrading air and land units. If you use your eastmost camp to build air units, and send those air units to attack the ring islands that still have enemy Zerg camps, you can build up a large number of ground units at the chokepoint leading to the main camp in the west.

Fig. 6-21. Make sure you have at least two Hatcheries at each resource node.

As the enemy Zerg armies build up, Guardians and Devourers attack you more and more frequently. Your Spore Colonies can't handle them all, so keep producing Mutalisks to defend your bases. The Zerg also like to land ground forces behind you with their Overlords, so a roaming group of Mutalisks used to hunt down and destroy enemy Overlords is an effective way to take out a large number of unfriendlies.

TIP

The enemy Zerg forces constantly send Hydralisks and Lurkers to harass you. Important: Keep at least one Overlord with each group at all times. You'll need them often to spot burrowed Lurkers.

After you've researched all upgrades and have a large attack force massed, you're ready to assault the main bases. Early in the mission, your objective changes from destroying enemy Zerg to killing all Terran Scientists. You'll find the Scientists in the Terran camp in the middle of the west edge of the map.

To reach the Terrans, you must eliminate the Zerg base in the northwest or southwest corner. Although you could overwhelm the enemy Zerg with a large number of Zerglings and Hydralisks, you'll make better progress with Ultralisks and Hydralisks. Because you have at least three resource patches from which to draw minerals, you should have enough to build several groups of Ultralisks. Guardians also are useful when attacking the main base.

After you destroy the Zerg camp, you can regroup to attack the Terrans. A number of Zerg units appear to be imprisoned in the Terran base. They remain passive during the mission, so you needn't destroy them.

Fig. 6-22. Terran Scientists wander around the base. Terminate them with extreme prejudice.

The Terran base is accessible only via a bridge on either side, making for a very difficult chokepoint. Rather than fight your way across the bridge, rush your units to the open spaces on the other side before letting them engage. You must move at least three or four groups of units into the Terran base to clear a safe zone on the other side of the bridge. If you let your units attack the Terrans as they move they'll stop fighting and block the bridge. The rest of your forces will be useless as they wait for the few on the bridge to inch forward or die.

Have your Guardians eliminate the Missile Turrets quickly, because you'll need to move your Overlords into the area of the Terran base to spot Lurkers. Remember, another whole enemy Zerg army beyond the Terrans awaits their chance to kill you. It's unnecessary to attack the second Zerg camp, but be prepared to defend against attackers from it.

When all 30 UED Scientists are dead, the Terrans lose control of the Zerg armies and you win the mission.

Resource Management

The resources along the north side of the map are slightly better than those in the south, so that's probably the best area to expand into. You must create units very quickly, so build at least two Hatcheries at each expansion base. There's only one Vespene Geyser on either side of the map, so gas will be a limiting factor. Build an Extractor as soon as you've built your Hatcheries and use at least three Drones per geyser to harvest gas.

Mission 7: Drawing of the Web

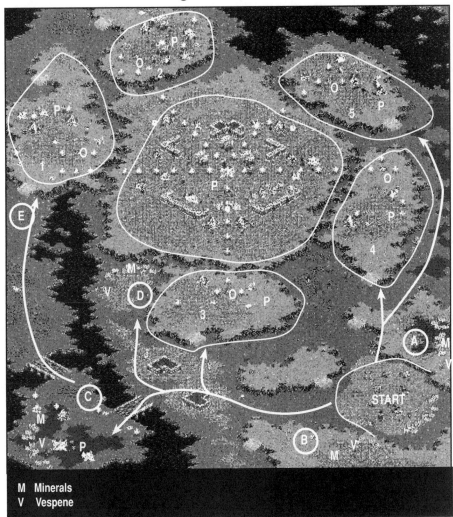

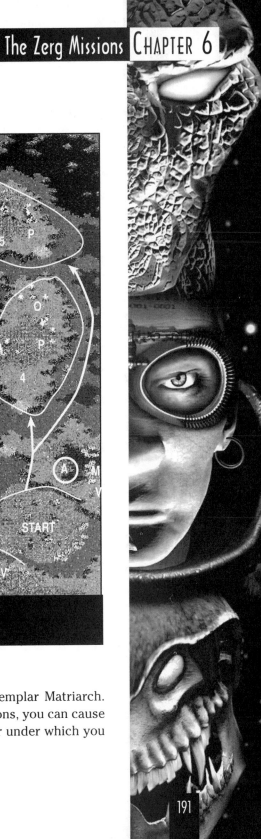

M Minerals
V Vespene

Fig. 6-23. Map of Zerg Mission 7

Kerrigan wants to return to Shakuras to steal the Dark Templar Matriarch. Although the Matriarch is well defended with Photon Cannons, you can cause a fluctuation in the power grid to provide the perfect cover under which you can whisk away the Matriarch.

Mission Objectives

▼ Duran must survive.
▼ Get Duran to each Zerg beacon.

Special Units

Duran

Battle Strategy

You begin this mission in the map's lower-right corner with a fairly substantial base. But that doesn't mean you can relax. Capture areas A and B immediately, and fortify them with Sunken and Spore Colonies as soon as you can. Keep fortifying these areas as you build up your resources and climb the tech tree.

TIP

The enemy uses plenty of Dark Templars in this mission, so you'll need Detector units to spot them.

Your goal is to get Duran to each of five beacons that are situated around the map in Protoss outposts. Unfortunately, you have no access to air units in this mission (other than Overlords), so you must find a way to defeat the enemy without the air support. Groups of Dark Templars will attack your base often, so keep your Overlords near entry points so your units can spot them.

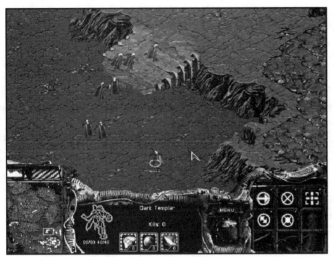

Fig. 6-24. Keep an eye out for Dark Templars. They'll attack from time to time when you're not looking.

Once your starting base and the expansion bases in areas A and B are secure, build up a force of Zerglings and Hydralisks (24 of each) to sweep over the Protoss base in Area C. This is the last area of resources you should need to capture to complete this mission. If you *do* need more minerals or Vespene, you can also easily capture Area D. When Area C is secure, move your forces up to Area E and build a Nydus Canal connecting you to your home base. This will make your efforts far easier when you go after beacons 1 and 2.

When attacking the areas surrounding the Beacons, keep the supply of units flowing. Attacking with four groups of 10 Hydralisks and 24 Zerglings isn't unheard of, so be aggressive right off the bat or you could end up losing an entire strike force. While your attacks on beacons 1 and 2 are underway, the main Protoss base is likely to launch an attack on your main base. You can repel these attacks, but be aware that Duran is often the target of these attacks, and if Duran dies the mission ends.

Fig. 6-25. Build Nydus Canals to channel your units to the battle area quickly.

After Duran activates beacons 1 and 2, do the same to beacons 3, 4, and 5. You must move slowly and attack with overwhelming forces every time you attack. Because there are no air units for you to use. Put those extra resources to good use by ensuring that your units are fully upgraded and by building Ultralisks. The Defiler can also be a great weapon in your arsenal, weakening enemy positions before you move in to overtake them in a frenzy of shield hits and blood.

Once you've managed to activate all five beacons with Duran, you've won! Now it's on to Mission 8.

Resource Management

The most important aspect of resource management in this mission involves capturing and securing areas A and B(complete with their own Hatcheries). Ultimately you'll probably need to draw at least some of the resources out of areas C and D, but this will depend on your tactical abilities and how many units you're losing when fighting to get Duran to the Beacons.

Your starting base and areas A and B are relatively easily defended, especially if you have Overlords nearby to spot for Dark Templars. Since your defensive position is a reasonable one, take your time to research all unit abilities and acquire all upgrades before you attempt any attacks.

Mission 8: To Slay the Beast

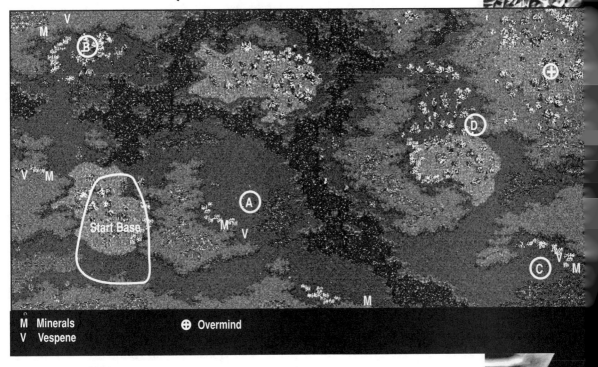

M Minerals
V Vespene

⊕ Overmind

Fig. 6-26. Map of Protoss Mission 8

Kerrigan and her Zerg minions have enlisted the aid of the Protoss to destroy the Overmind. However, the UED will provide ample resistance. You must find a way to battle through both the UED and the Overmind's forces if you're to get your Dark Templars to the Overmind and destroy it.

Mission Objectives

▼ Destroy the Overmind with the Dark Templar (you must be able to have Dark Templar).

Special Units

Dark Templar
Two Gateways and a Templar Archives

Battle Strategy

Your enemies on this level will hit you harder than ever and they'll never stop trying to take back any base you take from them. Any resource nodes captured from the enemy will have to be fortified strongly or you risk losing to the opposing force. In this level, you cannot afford a light attack against the enemy because that will just stir up a hornet's nest of aggression. Strike hard and fast or not at all.

NOTE

This mission is one of the most difficult missions in the game. You'll fight joint Terran/Zerg forces, and they'll be used against you to great effect. You'll face Guardians being healed by Medics, Goliaths and Hydralisks attacking side by side, and waves of Valkyries and Devourers together forming the strongest anti-air combination you can face.

You must protect your Gateways/Pylons/Templar Archives at all times; if you lose all your Dark Templars and the ability to make Dark Templars, you lose the mission. The computer will be sneaky at times, and will send Tanks to your Gateways and Templar Archives when you're not looking, so make sure you have strong air and ground defenses around those buildings.

Fig. 6-27. Protecting your base is critical in the early stages.

Start out by building a strong economy while getting your defenses going immediately, on both ends of your base. You'll get hit by both the white and the orange forces fairly early in the game, so increase the defenses at your main base right away. Move an Overlord and a Dark Templar to each end of your base and split up your initial groups of Hydralisks and Zerglings to defend the entrances.

NOTE

You'll probably lose some towns as waves of the enemies come at you. Just rebuild and keep pushing forward, and you'll see victory. The key in this level is always to protect your expansions and rebuild their defenses when they're destroyed.

As soon as you can, drop a couple of Sunken Colonies and a Spore Colony at each end of your base. Prepare to replace your Sunken Colonies as they're killed; there will be early attacks by Infested Terrans who will destroy your Sunken Colonies easily. You may also want to build Dark Templars for defense, as they start the mission fully upgraded and are sure death against any enemy without a Detector handy. Put any Dark Templars you build on patrol just outside your protective line of Sunken Colonies. This makes it much tougher for an enemy attack to succeed.

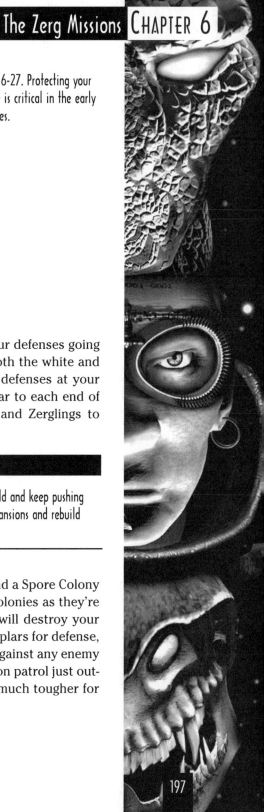

Fig. 6-28. Be sure to upgrade your Hydralisks before you venture forth.

As you build up to attack the first enemy area, get all three upgrades for your Hydralisks, and get the ranged attack and armor upgrades rolling, as well. Don't forget to get the Pneumatized Carapace (Extra Speed) upgrade for your Overlords at the Hive, because your Overlords will get chased around a lot during this mission, and you want to give them a chance to get away. You'll need another Hatchery in your main base, as well, to build the large numbers of Hydralisks this level demands.

After weathering a few attacks and once your economy is going strong, get out a fairly large number of Hydralisks with Lurker support to remove the enemy base in Area A. Twenty-four Hydralisks with four to six Lurkers as support should be more than enough to clean out Area A, but you'll want the extra troops there to hold it. The enemy will drop troops there all mission long, trying to take it back. Also, in this assault you want to include some Overlords (with the Speed upgrade) to keep a lookout for enemy Lurkers that will drop at your doorstep.

At this point, you should hunker down and build a Hatchery to mine resources from Area A. Although you should build a few Spore Colonies there for air defense (and as Detectors), you'll primarily defend this area with all the troops left over from the initial attack on the base. You can be sure that the computer will come calling more than once. Once the area is secure, and you've begun to mine this base, you should turn your eyes northward to Area B.

TIP

As you gather your forces for a push north, make sure to build a Queen's Nest, and then upgrade your Lair to a Hive. You'll need this to upgrade your Hydralisks to Level 3 armor and attack.

To attack Area B, send the same sized group you sent after Area A—24 or so Hydralisks with Lurker support. Don't pull these units from defending Area A. You'll need them there. Make new ones. Send your troops north and watch the white town crumble. You must leave the units there, as the enemy will try to take this town from you, as well. Keep your units away from the lava cliffs. Enemy Guardians will make short work of any ground unit that strays too close to the edge.

You now hold a complete (if very large) island. You'll need to go to the air to assault the Overmind's island. Make sure all your expansions on the eastern edge of the island are well defended with 12–24 Hydralisks and a Lurker or two for support.

Your next task is to set up an expansion at the resource area in Area C. You must build a Nydus Canal in your main base, but don't place the other end, yet. Then build 12 or so Hydralisks and a couple of Drones and put them in an Overlord headed for Area C. Once they arrive, drop off the Hydralisks and kill the few Lurkers hiding at the resource node, then build a Hatchery when you're done.

Fig. 6-29. Building a Nydus Canal from your home base to Area C will make your life easier.

199

Once the Hatchery is complete, select the Nydus Canal you just built and place the other end in your new base in Area C. Be sure to defend the area as you've been defending your other areas.

Time to prepare for the assault on Area D. You'll need as many Queens as you can manage to take care of troublesome enemy units. Also, bring in half a dozen or so Ultralisks to lead the charge and to absorb the bulk of the damage, as well as a large number of Hydralisks to clean up the town and take care of the air units.

TIP

When you go after the Overmind in Area B, first bring in your Queens and use Spawn Broodling on as many of the Tanks, Ultralisks and Defilers as you can. This will make the assault much easier.

When you begin your assault, lead with Ultralisks and follow with Hydralisks. The enemy probably will cast Dark Swarm to protect himself, but if you get your Ultralisks inside fast, this can be turned to your advantage. This is the game's most difficult assault. If it fails, you should still be in a strong position with plenty of resources to send a second wave similar to the first.

After you break through the defenses in Area D, wipe out the entire area. All that remains now is to assault the plateau, where the Overmind resides. Once more, use Queens to parasite one or more enemy units on the plateau, and then use Spawn Broodling on whatever you find most offensive. After you've thinned out the enemies, deposit another round of Hydralisks and Ultralisks on the ledge on the south side of the plateau and overrun Area D. Make sure you have lots of Overlords to cover your advance because the Overmind is virtually ringed by Lurkers.

Resource Management

You start with a Hatchery and a Lair. Use both to build up a large body of Drones to do your mining. When in doubt, build more Drones until you have about two workers per mineral you're mining (or about 16 Drones mining minerals and three to four Drones harvesting gas). You must build your economy quickly in this mission so you can get your war machine moving before the really strong enemy attacks begin.

Before you launch your first attack against orange Zerg, search behind your base to the west. You'll find a small expansion against the edge of the map. Send a Drone there and build a Hatchery as soon as possible. Harvesting from a second geyser may be a necessary requirement for a strong Zerg air offense. Make sure you have a Spore Colony or two there, just in case.

After taking out the orange base next door, search to the south of this base and build a Hatchery at the mineral node there. Build at this base only if you're running short of minerals, though, because the computer will try and take it from you. You'll spend units and time defending this town, as well.

Now just remember to keep rebuilding if a town is destroyed and to get your Drones moved to a new mineral area when the one they're harvesting is exhausted.

Mission 9: The Reckoning

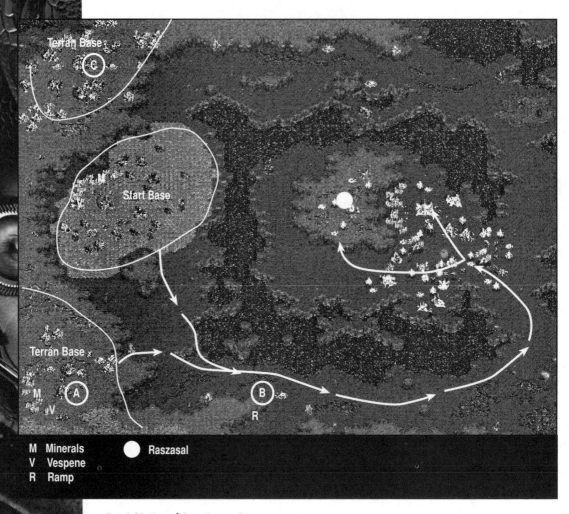

Fig. 6-31. Map of Zerg Mission 9

Zeratul has captured the Matriarch and imprisoned her in a Stasis Cell on the planet Char. Kerrigan has sent her remaining Broods to Char to eliminate the Protoss and Terran forces and reclaim the Protoss Matriarch for the Zerg cause.

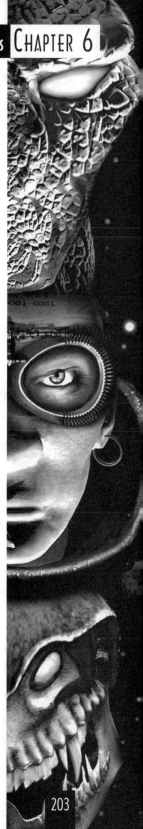

Mission Objectives

▼ Destroy the Protoss base within 30 minutes.
▼ Recover the Matriarch and Zeratul.

Special Units

Zeratul
Kerrigan
Raszagal

Battle Strategy

This key to this level is speed and your ability to harvest resources while conducting attacks as efficiently as possible. Begin by having your Hive and Hatchery build two Hydralisks each; at the same time, move your Guardians south. In Area A you'll find a Terran base you must destroy. You'll need the minerals and gas at this base, so get moving posthaste.

Move to the ramp in Area B and take out the Siege Tank. Then send your Ultralisk into the base, followed immediately with everything else you start with—all the Zerglings, one of the two Lurkers, and all the Hydralisks, including the four you just made. This force should be enough to take out the base. Once this is done, spawn a Hatchery there immediately.

Fig. 6-32. Taking Area A quickly is critical, so waste no time.

At this point, you must gather resources as quickly as possible. Assign two Drones per mineral patch at each base, and four Drones per Assimilator.

NOTE

Make sure you get all Hydralisk, Ultralisk, air unit, and Overlord upgrades. You'll especially need the Overlord Speed and Transporting upgrades, because part of the enemy base lies atop a cliff and you must get your troops up there. Don't forget to research the Melee Attack, Missile Attack, and Armor upgrades at the Evolution Chamber, as well.

Now, begin preparing the large Hydralisk hammer you'll use to crack the Protoss base. You must build 48 Hydralisks and a support force of five Guardians. You'll need at least five Ultralisks to lead the charge and take the brunt of the damage from enemy Reavers and Psionic Storm. As you build your attack force, use your expansion Area A as a staging area, foiling attacks from the Terrans in Area C.

Group a bunch of your Overlords and send them in to spot the enemy Dark Templars. You can go whenever you feel ready, but you should assume it'll take at least five minutes to clean out the base, so try to attack somewhere around the 10-minute mark.

TIP

If you can defeat this mission with at least five minutes remaining on the timer you'll get access to the *secret level*!

Before you send your full attack group along the path that runs across the bottom edge of the map, you should clear the area of the Siege Tanks that are stationed on top of the overlooking ridges, as well as the Bunker that guards the midpoint of your intended route. Guardians are your best unit to use here because you can kill all of this opposing force without losing a unit. After the way is clear, move your assault corps so that they are just outside the Protoss Base.

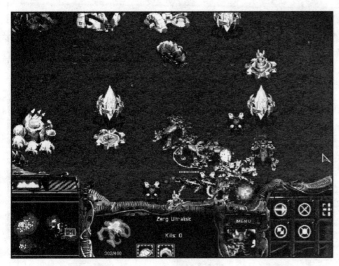

Fig. 6-33. Send your Ultralisks in first to absorb the Reavers' attacks.

As the attack begins, send in the Ultralisks, followed closely by the Hydralisks. The Ultralisks should draw most of the Reaver fire and Psionic Storms, thus sparing the Hydralisks. You must use your Guardians to pick off enemy Reavers and Templars trying to engage your Hydralisks as they make their way through the base. After defenses have folded, send the Guardians to destroy the cannons up on the plateau, while the Hydralisks destroy everything left in the main area. If you have no more Guardians left, you'll need to transport some Hydralisks up to the plateau with your Overlords and let them finish the deed.

Resource Management

Getting gas is your primary concern here, and thus you should have your Drones collecting Vespene immediately. Mine gas on the expansion once you take it, as well. You'll still need minerals to buy more Drones, so don't neglect working the mineral fields during the early stages of the mission.

Secret Mission: Dark Origin

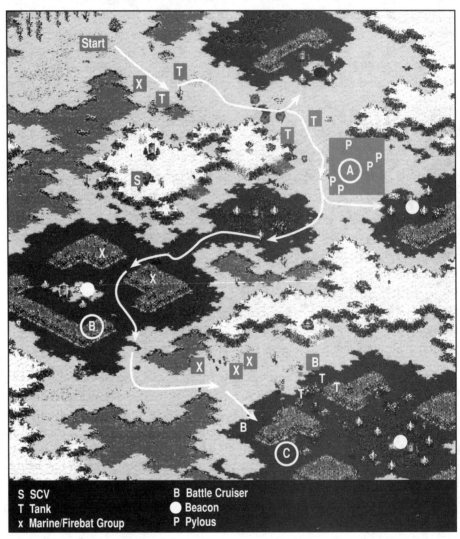

S SCV	**B** Battle Cruiser
T Tank	● Beacon
x Marine/Firebat Group	**P** Pylous

Fig. 6-34. Map of Secret Mission

You'll get this secret bonus mission automatically when you complete Zerg Mission 9 with more than five minutes remaining on the 30-minute counter.

Zeratul is despondent because Protoss fleets are scattered across the galaxy and the Matriarch has been sacrificed. However, if Zeratul can find Artanis and his warriors, the Protoss may be able to return to Shakuras.

Strange energy signatures emanating from the Dark Mood may indicate that Artanis is there, and Zeratul intends to find him.

Mission Objectives

▼ Investigate the energy signatures.
▼ Zeratul must survive.

Special Units

Stasis Cell Prison

Battle Strategy

You've made it to the secret bonus mission, but just because it's secret doesn't mean it's all fun and games. This mission has its own special challenges you must overcome to make it all the way through. You begin in the upper-left corner of the map with Zeratul, four Dark Archons (complete with Mind Control), and a pair of Dragoons.

Fig. 6-35. Use your Dark Archons to grab these Siege Tanks right off the bat.

Move your troops cautiously south, until you can just see some Terran Marines. Send Zeratul forward to improve your vision until the two Siege Tanks come into view. Then use your Dark Archons to mind-control both Tanks simultaneously. (You may well capture a Science Vessel at the same time.) As you continue moving south, you'll encounter a pair of Medics that would also serve your cause well. Mind-control the Medics, too.

TIP

Mind Control is your best friend in this mission. In fact, the folks at Blizzard have done a great job of making this a mission where you can mind-control all kinds of enemy units, so use the Mind Control ability liberally.

Area A is well defended by a Siege Tank and a row of Photon Cannons. The Siege Tank is easy to capture with Mind Control, but the Photon Cannons cannot fall victim to the powers of your Dark Archons. If you get close enough to the Cannons with a Science Vessel, you'll get the attention of a Battlecruiser: if you're smart, it will soon be yours, as well. When you have the Battlecruiser, take out the Pylons in front of the Photon Cannons to disable them.

Once you've cleared Area A and further augmented your forces through Mind Control, take time to have Zeratul examine the two beacons in this area.

Move cautiously toward Area B using your Science Vessel to spot for your Siege Tanks. If you don't have a Science Vessel, there's one near Area B that you can capture. There's an SCV near one of the Stasis Cells in Area B, as well; grab it so you can repair your Battlecruisers and Tanks as the mission progresses. Don't bother trying to Mind Control the groups of Marines on the platforms around Area B; instead, use your Siege Tanks to lay them waste.

Fig. 6-36. Grab this SCV so you can repair your captured Terran units.

Move through Area B (having Zeratul stop by the beacon), and then proceed south toward Area C. This is the map's most heavily defended area, but it will give you a chance to pick up some new units. There are three Battlecruisers, four Wraiths, three Siege Tanks, and even a Science Vessel you can capture, if you're careful. Move up slowly and use your Science Vessels to spot for your Siege Tanks and your Dark Archons. When you've secured a path through to the beacon in Area C, activate it to end the mission.

I won't give away the story line behind this mission. You can learn the ugly truth for yourself.

Resource Management

The only resources you must manage in this mission are your Dark Archons. Treat them with kid gloves, because they're your only means of building up your forces. You also have a small (and limited) amount of minerals and Vespene: when repairing Terran units, choose wisely.

Mission 10: Omega

M Minerals
V Vespene

Fig. 6-37. Map of Zerg Mission 10

You face three rather powerful forces that are determined to stop you by any means necessary. The UED expeditionary fleet led by Admiral Dugalle wants total control of this sector, and sees your control of the Overmind as a threat. Arcturus Mengsk and a coalition of interests in the Koprulu sector want you dead. Artanis and the Protoss fleet have come for revenge. They've taken up positions around you on your space platform: you must crush them once and for all.

Mission Objectives

▼ Destroy all enemy forces.

Special Units

None

Battle Strategy

You face three separate forces that pose very different challenges for the Zerg swarms. The UED to the north have considerable control of the air, in the form of Battlecruisers, Valkyries, and Goliaths. Mengsk's forces in the west rely on a rather brutal ground attack made up of Siege Tanks and infantry, backed with nuclear missiles. The Protoss to the southeast will use their psionic powers against you by bringing Templars, Dark Archons, Arbiters, and Corsairs to the fray.

Your starting base lies in the middle of the space platform with three ground entrances leading into your main stronghold. All three enemy forces will send considerable troops into your base early and hard, so fortify your holdings immediately. Enemy attacks can occur at any of the three entrances, so place many more Sunken Colonies to guard all the ways in.

As the game progresses you must build Spore Colonies, as well, to help defend against attacks from the air. A smaller force can guard the northern entrance, because you have a more defensible ramp there.

Fig. 6-38. Building up an early defensive matrix is critical to your survival in this mission.

Keep a mobile force of Hydralisks and Zerglings ready to reinforce your static defenses at a moment's notice. You must begin producing Mutalisks, as well, as a mobile reserve. Siege Tanks and Reavers have a longer range than your Sunken Colonies, and you'll need the Mutalisk's fast air attack to break up their attacks.

You must make a difficult choice: you must attack one of three enemy forces, but each offers a different challenge.

TIP

Research Burrowing, as well, for several reasons. Burrowed Zerglings and Lurkers make awesome early warning devices, and you can plan effective ambushes using Lurkers and burrowed Hydralisks along the paths the enemy ground units take to your base. If one of your expansions is overrun, burrowing also allows you to save many Drones you'd otherwise lose.

Attacking Mengsk's bases to the west with ground troops is difficult. His Siege Tanks, Marines, Firebats, and Ghosts can decimate Zerglings, Hydralisks, and even Ultralisks quickly. Defilers and Queens are a must for supporting any ground attack with their Dark Swarm and Spawn Broodling abilities. Engage Mengsk with a sizable air force, including Guardians and Devourers—but don't assume he's defenseless in the air. He controls numerous Wraiths and Science Vessels that can disrupt your air attacks, and the enormous number of stimmed Marines can chew up Mutalisks quickly.

Remember to bring in Overlords to spot the Wraiths, Ghosts, and Spider Mines. In taking out Mengsk, you eliminate two key threats—Siege Tanks and Nukes. Both can cause real problems when you are trying to defend your resources and the Hive clusters.

Fig. 6-39. Take on Mengsk's forces using Guardians and Devourers.

The UED to the north are more vulnerable to strong ground attacks, but they compensate with a powerful air defense. You'll need a strong Hydralisk force to take down the defending Battlecruisers, but Zerglings (with the Adrenal Glands upgrade) and Ultralisks also will be a big help in taking down ground-based defenses. The Defiler's Dark Swarm ability can quickly turn the tide, as the UED has few units here that can affect your melee attackers operating under the cloud of a Dark Swarm. Taking out the UED is a priority, if you're having real trouble defending your Overlords from marauding Valkyries.

You can attack your final opponent from both ground and air, but the defensive abilities of the Protoss are quite nasty. Dark Archons will mind-control key units, or maelstrom entire masses of Zerg units at once. Templars, with their Psionic Storms, are always a danger, and both Arbiters and Corsairs can break up attacks in a frighteningly effective way using Stasis Field and Disruption Web. Once the Protoss are gone you'll no longer have to worry about Corsairs disrupting your Sunken and Spore Colonies, and you will have put an end to their powerful attacks

Fig. 6-40. Dark Archons will mind-control your powerful units, if you're not careful.

With this knowledge of enemy defenses, you can decide which enemy to attack. When you do engage the enemy, make sure you do so with overwhelming force. Once one of the enemy bases takes serious damage, you can expect all three sides to send units to try and thwart your attack. You must destroy each base quickly and decisively, or you'll fight what seems like endless streams of reinforcements. Fighting a long war of attrition and enemy skirmishes is a sure route to defeat. Just remember to keep a reserve available when you send in your assault waves. Nothing is worse than having to break off a successful attack to save one of your outposts from being overrun by the enemy.

When you destroy the last enemy force, victory is yours.

Resource Management

You begin the level with large quantities of both minerals and gas, but you'll quickly find that even the resources of your main platform aren't enough. You must expand. The area just south of you is the most logical first expansion to make. No enemy forces guard the area, although both Mengsk's forces and the Protoss can attack any Hive cluster you start there easily. Be prepared. Securing additional resources is far more difficult, but may be necessary.

Upgrade your troops quickly to match the power of your opponents. Large numbers of Guardians, Devourers, or Ultralisks can be rather expensive. The resource areas with the least resistance lie toward the northwest corner of the map. Although the UED has a major base in that corner, there are several smaller areas along the way that aren't heavily defended.

Multiplayer Games

Battle.net™

To use Blizzard's free multiplayer service, you must have a connection to the Internet. If you have a dial-up account that uses a modem to connect to the Internet, make sure you connect successfully before starting *Starcraft*. This saves time and frustration, especially if you must troubleshoot problems.

From the main *Starcraft* screen, select Multiplayer and then Battle.net. A message indicates the game is searching for the fastest server; then you'll see the login screen. To create a new account, follow the onscreen instructions; otherwise, enter the user name and password for your existing account. Once you're logged on, you'll find yourself in one of many chat rooms.

Fig. 7-01. Battle.net allows you to pit your *Brood War* skills against those of players from around the world.

In the chat room, you can meet friends for a prearranged game or find other players to battle. To join a game, hit the Join button and pick a game from the list, or type the name and password of a game you've previously agreed on with friends. To create a game, hit the Create button and type in a game name and password (optional). Using a password restricts entry to your game to those players who know the password. If you create a game, you may select the number of players, their species, and the map you'll play on.
You can only select your own species, but you *can* choose whether or not there are computer players and how many slots remain open for other players to potentially join.

Updates

Blizzard updates its game software periodically. When you sign onto Battle.net, the network determines whether you need to upgrade. If you do, it sends you the newest version of the game automatically. After the new software has downloaded, the game restarts on its own and applies the upgrade. You must have the most recent version of *Starcraft* or *Starcraft: Brood War* to play games on Battle.net.

Troubleshooting

The Internet can be a great way to play games interactively, or it can sometimes be like trying to communicate using tin cans and a string. If you have problems getting *Starcraft* to work over Battle.net, keep these points in mind:

1. You must have a 32-bit connection to the Internet. It's difficult to know whether your connection is a true 32-bit link, but if you have any doubt, just remember that most connections are 32-bit connections.

> ▼ If you use Dial-Up Networking to connect, you're most likely getting a 32-bit connection.
> ▼ If, however, you use a terminal program or a third-party dialer, you'll probably get only a 16-bit connection, and be unable to play *Starcraft* on Battle.net.
> ▼ If you play other games on the Internet, you'll probably have no trouble with *Starcraft*.

2. The reason you need a 32-bit connection is that the game uses universal datagram packets (UDPs) to send game information back and forth as you play. If your ISP won't admit these types of packets, you won't be able to play on Battle.net. This is important to know if you use an account at your place of business or educational institution; often these types of ISP don't allow such game packets through.

3. If your connection is too slow, your game will be jumpy and unreliable. Your modem's (or other connection method's) line speed together with Internet conditions determine the speed of your connection.

Is the Connection Good?

Latency is a major factor in online gaming. In simple terms, latency is a measure of how long it takes your computer to communicate with the host computer running the game. Low latency is good, because it means the two computers communicate quickly. High latency is bad, because it means there's a significant delay between the events happening on the host computer and what you see onscreen.

In the Battle.net chat room, the latency bar next to your name displays your latency to the other player. In the list of games to join, your latency bar shows your latency to each game, which may differ from your latency to Battle.net. Short green bars mean you have very little latency. Longer yellow or red bars mean you've got significant latency.

The Multiplayer Experience

Multiplayer gaming differs significantly from single-player. For one thing, single-player missions are "set," and multiplayer affairs are more like stories yet to be written. For another, human opponents provide an entirely different kind of gaming experience from computer AI.

Multiplayer gaming also has more of an element of surprise, especially when you're playing with three or more opponents. Will your allies turn on you? Will the closest enemy ally with another player to crush you? The permutations that can occur in multiplayer games are mind-boggling, making multiplayer gaming the "spice" that keeps *Starcraft* interesting for months instead of days.

The Human Factor

Humans provide much deeper and more challenging opponents than even the best computer AI. The rewards of playing against humans are many, and will make you a better *Starcraft* player, greatly improving your strategy skills.

What makes multiplayer action so much better? There are a few theories about that.

THE BRAIN

Sure, Deep Blue can mentally outmuscle Gary Kasparov at chess, but those of us with everyday PCs on our desks don't have much to worry about. The human brain is still far and away the superior thinker when pitted against the gaming AI. *Starcraft*'s AI is excellent, but once you know how to defeat a scenario, that's the end. However, when a human is at the enemy controls, you

have no idea what will happen next. A human is a smart and unpredictable being, and that's what makes him or her such a great adversary.

Sure, you may understand human tendencies—a human player likes to build 35 Siege Tanks, for example—but in the end, you never really know what a human will do.

THE GRUDGE

Losing to a human usually makes you feel worse than losing to a computer. The resulting grudge will inspire you to try harder the next time you face off. Many of this book's best strategies came from two humans bashing on each other in a multiplayer game of *Starcraft: Brood War*.

GLOATING

The feeling of pride you get from defeating your friends can be a big motivator for improving your gaming skills. The satisfaction that comes from winning a multiplayer *Starcraft* game ranks much higher than beating the computer's AI.

TAUNTING

For many, defeating a human usually means a chance to rub it in. Sure it's juvenile, but taunting your enemies can throw off their game. Although it can backfire, boasting can inspire crippling doubt in your opponent. If you get a message that says, "I hope your flank's protected," does it really mean that enemy will attack your flank? Or is the enemy just messing with your mind?

Multiplayer Tips

If you're new to the real-time strategy genre, or just want to brush up on your skills, consider the following helpful multiplayer tips.

Speed

The first thing you'll probably notice about your human opponents is the speed with which they get their act in gear. You might still be tinkering with your base, defenseless, when suddenly a horde of enemies comes knocking on your door. This is especially common when your opponent(s) plays Zerg: those cheap, easy-to-build Zerglings can cause havoc in the game's early stages.

Stay fast and focused during the game's first few minutes. Build only the essentials and always keep an eye on defense. Don't build extraneous stuff until you've got a strong production chain and several combat units. And make sure you get lots of resource harvesters (such as SCVs) into action as quickly as possible. The more of them you have, the faster you can build your war machine.

Keep Your Scan Going

You should play *Starcraft* in a high energy state, always looking around the map for new areas to explore, new units to build, new resources to exploit, and new enemies to corner and kill. Never sit to watch and wait for units to be completed or to reach their destinations. Time spent idly will cost you the game when you play against skilled opponents.

Establish a rhythm of scanning your units, building new ones, strengthening defenses, and mining new resources. Developing a methodical way of consistently reviewing your units can increase productivity and awareness considerably. Keep your mouse pointer busy.

Fig. 7-02. Don't be afraid to build plenty of gathering units (SCVs/Probes/Drones). The more you have, the faster you gather.

For example, if you find a new area with resources to exploit, instead of waiting for a new Drones to be built and to move to the new area, send existing Drones now and have the new ones take over the old ones' activities. Also, don't let your buildings sit idle. If you're running too low on resources to build new units continually, increase the number of Drones/Probes/SCVs mining for mineral and gas (or find new sources of these resources).

Defending

Don't let your guard down. When you send a task force of soldiers to attack your enemy, keep some in reserve to defend your bases, and be sure to build a decent network of defensive structures. Clear-thinking players realize the best time to attack an enemy base is when the enemy is attacking yours. This forces opponents to divide their attention—and their troops.

Establish second and third bases as soon as you can. If your opponent takes out your only base, the game is over. If your opponent finds an auxiliary base and destroys it, you're still in the game and can strike back.

Fig. 7-03. Make sure you have multiple bases, especially the Zerg, whose units come straight from the Hatcheries.

Having a large number of cheap units is the most efficient way to wage war in the beginning and middle parts of the game, but once you've researched the tech tree fully you'll need to create more powerful defensive units. Don't neglect your research!

Attacking

Once you commit to an attack, don't back down. Keep producing and sending units to attack until you break the opposition. If it looks like you aren't making progress, don't give up! You'll win, because most enemy players will be too preoccupied with defense to mount an attack of their own and come after you. Too often players attack with one or two waves of units and then give up, even though they're very close to breaking their enemies' backs.

It's helpful to build attacking units near your opponent's base. That way you can send reinforcements as soon as they're completed. *Starcraft*'s (and *Brood War*'s) ability to queue up production and set "focal" (rally) points for units is a great aid for players mounting a sustained attack.

Fig. 7-04. It's tempting to try to win with lots of one unit, but this strategy won't work against experienced players.

Although it can be tempting to make a couple of large groups of your most powerful unit, this can be risky if your opponent knows how to counter that unit. Therefore, it's important to attack with *at least* two unit types. Include one unit type that can attack air targets and one that can hit ground units. This way your attack force can't be wiped out by one or two defenders it can't even touch.

As in real-life battle, your initial attack probably will be most effective if it comes from two or more directions at once. This tactic forces the enemy to divide his defenders and attention while your attackers pour in. Even if your other attacks are simple diversions, you'll make the enemy defend against them all.

Brood War New Unit Tricks

There are a few new units in *Starcraft: Brood War*. Not surprisingly there are a few new tricks and tips for each of these units. Scott Mercer from Blizzard Entertainment helped supply some of these insightful strategies for making the most of these new units.

Medic Tricks

▼ Keeping a Medic or two among the stream of workers gathering resources can help immensely if you're attacked by Wraiths, Mutalisks, or Scouts.

▼ Optical Flare can disrupt Reaver drops by blinding both the Shuttle and the Reaver.

▼ In a team game, a Zerg army with Medic backup for healing can be a potent combination.

▼ Restoration can remove a host of malicious effects, including Parasite, Plague, Ensnare, Lockdown, Irradiate, and Devourers' Acid Spores.

▼ Medics allow your Marines and Firebats to use Stimpacks liberally.

Valkyrie Tricks

▼ Valkyries can decimate groups of Overlords quickly if the Zerg player doesn't have them well-protected.

▼ Valkyries and Devourers working together are the game's most devastating anti-air combination. Devourers' Acid Spores will increase the damage inflicted by *each* missile that damages the target. Given the massive barrage of missiles launched with every Valkyrie attack, it won't take long to decimate enemy air targets.

▼ Valkyrie missiles do splash damage, so fire into large masses of enemy air units when you can to maximize the total damage done.

Lurker Tricks

▼ Burrow Lurkers at chokepoints you know enemy ground troops must cross.

▼ Place a few Lurkers around your resources to attack any enemy units dropped there. Lurkers also can devastate enemy workers.

▼ Placing Lurkers at key crossroads around the map not only can provide excellent reconnaissance, but the Lurker often can kill lone enemy scouting units.

▼ Lurkers excel at taking out waves of light infantry, especially Marines and Firebats.

Devourer Tricks

▼ Although you can use Devourers without any support, the Acid Spore effect makes following up Devourer attacks with a wave of Mutalisks particularly deadly. The Mutalisk's Glave Wurm (its main attack) can hit up to three targets, doing successively less damage as it bounces from target to target. Each Acid Spore will add one hit of damage to *any* attack the afflicted unit receives, so even the last hit of the Glave Wurm can do major damage if enough Acid Spores are on the target.

▼ Acid Spores also slow the affected unit's rate of fire. This is particularly brutal to units that already have long waits between attacks, such as Valkyries, Battlecruisers, and other Devourers.

Dark Archon Tricks

▼ Mind Control can be an excellent defense if you expect Reavers or other units to drop into your base soon. A successful mind-control of the Shuttle, Dropship, or Overlord not only gains you a new transport, but also whatever the transport is carrying!

▼ The Maelstrom ability is particularly effective against the Zerg, because all their units are biological. With Zerg units briefly frozen in place, you can use Psionic Storm on them with a nearby Templar and deal with the situation permanently.

▼ In a long game with many resources at your disposal, mind-controlling an SCV or Zerg Drone can increase your army's size dramatically. Although the expense of creating the entire tech tree for either race is nothing to sneer at, you can potentially have another 200 supply units to attack your enemies with. You also can create an army with the best units from more than one species.

▼ Feedback is easy to overlook, but at a cost of only 50 energy you can use Feedback quickly several times and often severely damage, if not kill, most units with an energy bar, including Wraiths, Science Vessels, Queens, Defilers, Templars, Battlecruisers, and Ghosts.

▼ If a Zerg player likes to parasite your units, mind-control the Queen, and then parasite the Zerg units instead!

Dark Templar Tricks

▼ Consider quickly building Templar Archives to begin production of Dark Templars. If you can attack a Terran or Protoss player before they have adequate Cloak detection, you can cause a great deal of havoc. Even if you attack with only one Dark Templar, your enemy often will overreact and spend more resources than necessary to defend against cloaked units.

▼ With their permanent cloaking ability, Dark Templars make excellent reconnaissance units. They also can disrupt incoming ground attacks, when placed well ahead of the rest of your defenses.

Corsair Tricks

▼ Disruption Web is an extremely powerful ability, and can make air attacks against enemy ground troops and defensive structures much easier. Be sure to get the energy upgrade for Corsairs. It allows a fully energized one to use Disruption Web twice before depleting its energy.

▼ Corsairs make awesome early spotters on island or large land maps. They're extremely fast units and much cheaper than Scouts. Scouts are much slower than Corsairs, as well, until you research their speed upgrade.

▼ Overlords make enticing targets for Corsairs, and you can punish quickly any Zerg player who likes to place Overlords all over the map to act as scouts.

Campaign Editor: Creating Worlds with StarEdit

One of the great things about both *Starcraft* and *Starcraft: Brood War* is that they ship with a campaign editor that allows you to create your own maps—entire *campaigns*, even, with story lines and characters. The only aspect of the *Starcraft* experience the average person can't include are Blizzard's spectacular cinematic sequences.

It would take an entire book to convey how to manage and exploit every nuance of *Starcraft: Brood War*'s campaign editor! So it seemed best to go straight to the source—Blizzard—and have tester Eric Dodds outline how to create a compelling map. Eric (with some help from Alen Lapidis) is largely responsible for the content that follows, and I'm grateful for their contributions.

For more in-depth coverage of the Campaign Editor, get *Starcraft™ Campaign Editor: Prima's Official Strategy Guide*. With it you'll become a master of creating awesome custom campaigns.

What Is It?

The *Starcraft: Brood War* campaign editor is a complex tool that enables the user to create completely functional single-player and multiplayer maps, as well as campaigns (stories that comprise a series of maps). Essentially, the editor is a user-friendly programming language that enables you to create new *Starcraft* realms.

The process of creating any campaign is complex. The single-player version of *Starcraft: Brood War* required the combined efforts of many skilled individuals working together over a period of months. But you don't have to spend months making a decent map or scenario that can be enjoyed over Battle.net or a home network.

Multiplayer Balancing

Perhaps the most important aspect of building multiplayer map is to ensure balance. That is, seeing to it the starting conditions for each player are relatively equal in terms of resources, units, and terrain. History shows that unbalanced maps die a quick death in the ring of public opinion.

Single-Player Balancing

A balanced single-player map forces players to use all their abilities to win, but it isn't so difficult that winning is impossible. There's a fine line between creating a computer opponent that's too tough and one that's too wimpy. A balanced map ensures players an engrossing, satisfying gaming experience.

Building Your Own Map

Before you start building a real map, try building a few simple ones to get a grasp of basic map design (doodads, triggers, locations, and so on). This practice saves time in the long run. Trying to make a complicated idea work before you've learned the ropes is never a good approach.

Remember, the map editor's online Help is very good. If you're confused, bring up online Help (press F1, or select Help from the Help menu) and you'll probably get an answer to your question.

To use all the cool triggers and locations, select the Use Map Settings game type when you start the game with the map. If you don't, you'll play on the terrain you've created, but with standard units, and none of your triggers or locations will work.

Steps for Building a Map

What follows is a basic walkthrough of some key components of map-building, such as placing doodads (little pieces of art) or triggers (linked events) throughout the map to add to the complexity and fun of your scenario. Creating a map can take days of work, so don't approached it as if it were a one- or two-hour project.

The following advice is far from a hard-and-fast road map, but it will help get you on course.

The Vocabulary of Campaign Editing

Trigger: Something that triggers an event. For example, you can tell the game to trigger 10 Marines to appear spontaneously once a player harvests more than 2000 gas units from a Vespene Geyser. There's no end to what you can make a trigger do, from generating enemy attacks to serving up a bit of story text.

Doodad: Little bits of artwork, such as skeletons, signs, and trees, laid out around the map for visual color. The exception is ramps, also included in the doodad menu.

Step One: Design the Map in Your Head

Come up with a basic idea before sitting down at the editor. Choose forces for each player and determine which special triggers you'll need to implement your idea. Go to the Help screens for triggers (select Help from the menu, go to the index, and check out triggers) and see if what you want to do can be done.

Eric's Triggers in "Gods of War"

I've decided on a scenario using three players. Each has a special power none of the others has. I want to call it "Gods of War" and create three special powers— one for each player—based on what I know about triggers and how they work.

The first player will have the ability to teleport around the map. I know the Moveto trigger allows me to move units around the map. Player 2 will be a warrior type and will get hero units after a given number of kills. A "kill counter" enables the map to count kills, and I can make suitable hero units. The third player will be the "horde player," with lots of weak units. I'll set up the map so that if this player has the fewest units, it will trigger the appearance of free Zerglings until Player 3 no longer has the fewest units. This is done using the "least" condition in the trigger menu.

Select the Tileset

The tileset is the basic palette of terrain types. Select New from the File menu to pop up a dialogue box that asks for the base tileset you want. Browse through and select the tileset that best fits your idea. You'll also select your map's basic overall terrain type here. Not all terrain types can accept structures, so select fundamental terrain types for your first maps (dirt, jungle, desert, and the like).

Eric's Tileset for "Gods of War"

The Jungle tileset best fits my idea for the "Gods of War" scenario, and there are several doodads in this tileset I want in my map. I select Jungle Tileset and then select Jungle for my basic terrain type, because that's how I want most of the map to look. I select a 128-by-128 tile map because I want the game to last just long enough to be interesting. This may be a little large for a three-player map, but 96-by-96 might be too small.

Set the Player Settings

To access this section, select Players from the menu bar, and then select Settings. The four main areas here allow you to play with the units and tech tree.

PROPERTIES

This area controls species and whether a person, computer, group of rescuable units, or neutral player controls each unit. Choose settings appropriate for your scenario. For "Gods of War," Eric sets players 1, 2, and 3 on Human. He sets players 4 through 8 to Neutral, because it's a three-player game with no computer players. Player 1 is Terran, Player 2 Protoss, and Player 3 Zerg. He ignores players 4 through 8; they won't be used.

UNITS

This area allows you to choose the units and structures each player has access to. For each player, you can select any unit and set it as unbuildable for that player. All players can build all units and buildings by default. To keep a player from building a specific unit or building, turn the units or buildings "off." To disable the global feature that allows all players access to all units, select a unit or building, and then uncheck the Enabled by Default box.

UPGRADES

Set starting levels and maximum level each player can attain for each upgrade. Researchable upgrades have a setting of zero if the upgrade isn't researched, or 1 if it is.

SPECIAL ABILITIES

Here you select the special abilities each player starts with—disabled, researched, or enabled (the default)—for every special ability for each species. Eric's teleporting player will get Recall automatically, because teleportation is that player's theme.

Set Forces

To assign each player a force, click on and drag the player's icon to the force you want. To add color, click on each force and name it. This also helps you remember which force does what when you assign triggers later.

Eric Sets the Forces

In the "Gods of War" scenario, I left Player 1 in Force 1 and named it "Warlord." I moved Player 2 to Force 2 and named it "Translocator." I moved Player 3 to Force 3 and named it "Master of the Horde." I moved the remaining players to the last force and left it nameless.

PLACE THE TERRAIN

Go to the Layer menu and select Terrain. A palette of the various terrain choices will come up. (Or click on the Terrain folder on the tool tree on the left side of the screen and select terrain types from a list.) Click on your selection in the palette or tool tree and paint the map with it, leaving room for units to move and place resource areas.

PLACE RAMPS

From the Layer menu, select Doodads. At this point the only doodads you want to place are ramps. Ramps can be placed only on the southeast or southwest angled cliffs (or walls), and then only where the wall is flat and the ground is appropriate for the given ramp.

You'll find ramps in the Cliff or Wall doodad selections and they are generally the last few doodads in their specific palette. Fire up Help and look up Ramps in the index for more information on placing them.

PLACE THE UNITS

Go to the Layer menu and select Unit Layer. The tool tree menu on the left side of the screen lists the players. Within each player's folder, you'll find unit folders by type—ground, air, and so on. Open one of these and click on the unit you want to place on the map.

Double-click on any unit you place to change its properties. These vary by unit: You can change how many Interceptors or Scarabs Carriers and Reavers start with, for example. You also can change a unit's starting hit percentage, and the amounts of minerals or gas a mineral field or Vespene Geyser contains.

Resources

Resources—Vespene Geysers and mineral fields—are among the first items you should place on the map. Make sure you place enough mineral fields and geysers at each starting location, and make sure each player has enough room to establish a base there. In a standard game, each player starts with five or six mineral fields, containing 1500 minerals each, and a gas vent with 5000 gas.

To change the starting allocation of resources, either place more of a resource type or double-click on the resource in the tool tree and change how many of that resource it provides. Remember, placing equal starting resources for each player is a fairly important factor in balancing a scenario.

The resources players receive at the start strongly influence the type of game they play. Giving them few starting mineral fields and Vespene Geysers forces them to expand to secondary towns early on. Giving them an abundance of Vespene Geysers and mineral fields allows them to camp and use their own starting towns for resource supplies throughout most of the game.

Choose a Starting Location

Use a special marker unit to select a starting location for each player. This unit tells the game where the player is when the game begins. Place some of that player's starting units near the starting location; otherwise, when the game starts the player will see only a black screen area. Each player must have a starting location before you can save the game (and certainly before you can run it).

Place Structures

Next, place each player's structures. Typically this means placing a Command Center, Nexus, or Hatchery on or near each player's starting location. Then place other structures as your design requires.

Each player starts with a hub for his base (Command Center, Nexus, or Hatchery) and a structure that provides additional supplies (Pylon, Supply Depot, or Overlord). This allows players to concentrate on building various types of units instead of wasting resources building supply units.

PLACE SPECIAL ITEMS

Special Items includes things such as the Terran player's Beacons, Flags, and Spider Mines. Beacons are useful for marking special locations. (For details, see "Create Locations.")

Eric's Special Placement

I need a number of special Beacons in "Gods of War." The Protoss player needs four to tell that player where his or her four teleports are. The Terran player needs a Beacon to mark where heroes will appear when his or her kills earn them. The Zerg player's Beacon will indicate where needed Zerglings will appear.

PLACE STARTING UNITS

Now place each player's starting units. A standard start provides each player with a few basic harvesting units. Add other units as your design dictates, but remember—you probably shouldn't start players with more units than their Psi/supplies/Command rating will support. That is, start your players with enough Supply Depots, Pylons, or Overlords to support their starting units.

CREATE LOCATIONS

Locations are special map areas tied directly to triggers. Because locations are invisible during gameplay, Beacons often are used to indicate location areas.

To create a location, select the Layer menu option and go to Locations. Now you can create a location anywhere you click on the map. Create a small

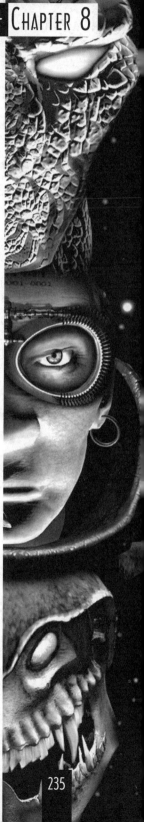

location; click on the map's corner boxes, holding the mouse button down as you drag it to change the location's size. When it's the size you want it, click on the center of the location and hold down the mouse button to drag it to where you want it to be. Double-click on the location to change its name. Try to name locations to reflect their functions, rather than "location 7, 8, 9," for example. This makes it easier to select the locations you want when you assign triggers. All this makes more sense after you've played with triggers a bit.

ASSIGN TRIGGERS

Triggers are a limited scripting language that allow you to have game events occur in response to the actions of one or more players. They're the campaign editor's heart and soul. They're what make it so powerful.

To create a new trigger, select the Scenarios menu option, and then select Triggers. A large dialogue box will come up listing default triggers. These control when a player wins or loses, and how much minerals and gas a player starts with.

Click on the New button for a list of players. Select the players you want the new trigger to affect, and then click Next to create the conditions that will set off the trigger.

Click on New to create a new conditional. (Use online Help to learn what each conditional does.) You must create at least one conditional to continue to the next screen. Choose from among a pull-down list of conditional templates. When you select a conditional, a statement will appear in the box below the list. Click on highlighted words to make the conditional work in your specific instance. The highlighted area will allow you to select the type of unit you want to test for, or where the player must arrive to set off the conditional. You can make it so a player must meet more than one conditional to activate a trigger.

After creating all the trigger conditionals you want, click on Next to set up the action(s) that take place when they're met. These appear in the same format as conditionals. Actions are what happens after a player meets your conditions. Typical actions are "Player gets 100 mineral units," or "Create a Marine for the player at (a certain location)." Select your actions the way you selected your conditionals.

When you're done with actions, you've created a trigger.

Eric's Triggers for "Gods of War"

TERRAN WHO GETS HEROES FOR KILLS
Player 1
Condition: if player one kills x units
Action: create unit "Hero Y" at location "Terran hero arrival area"

PROTOSS TRANSPORT LOCATIONS
Player 2
Condition: if player two brings a unit to location "teleporter x"
Action: move all units at location "teleporter x" to location "teleporter x destination"

THE ZERG ZERGLING HORDE
Player 3
Condition: if player three has the least amount of units
Action: create a Zergling at location "Zergling arrival area"

ADD DOODADS

Doodads are the little bits of art that spice up your map, make it look interesting, and give it flavor. Select Doodads from the Layers menu to bring up a doodad palette. To place a doodad, select a terrain type from the pull-down menu bar at the top of the palette. Move the slider bar next to the doodad icon up and down to scroll through the doodads. Click on the doodad you want and click on the map to place it.

Some doodads are flat and units can walk over them; others aren't flat and units must walk around them. Which is which can be obvious, but sometimes you must figure it out on your own. Note, too, that trees affect combat. A unit in the trees has only a 70 percent chance of taking a hit, so placing trees can create interesting strategic possibilities.

CREATE A MISSION BRIEFING

Focus your briefings either toward the player or among portrait characters. A built-in transmission trigger is designed specifically to time portrait talking time and text displayed to the length of the audio track (.wav file), so both are presented fluently.

Alternatively, you can display only a talking portrait and text. Remember that .wav files increase a map file's size, and usually briefing .wavs are largest. To display text-based dialog, use the following trigger order:

```
Portrait Slot # ON
{
Talking Portrait Slot #
Display Text
Wait
}
```

Because you want to keep the portraits open until the end of a conversation, you'll probably want to hold off on disabling slots until the end of the conversation to keep it flowing smoothly. Make sure talking time, text time, and wait time all match. You may need to toy around with timing a bit to present the effect you want.

It's good practice to present players with mission objectives first, so the lower-left corner isn't left empty and so they don't miss the goals.

End the briefing with a one-line statement saying the briefing is over, and then turn all port slots off.

Experiment!

This brief look into the complex workings of the campaign editor is only a small sampling of what you can do using this tool. To become an expert, experiment, use the online Help, look at how triggers are used in other maps, check out *Starcraft Campaign Editor: Prima's Official Strategy Guide,* and don't stop until you've made the epic scenario or campaign of all time!

Appendix A: Unit Tables

Protoss Unit Table

Unit Name	Minerals	Vespene Gas	Supply	Hit Points	Shield	Ar
Arbiter	100	350	4	200	150	
Archon	100	300	4	10	350	
Carrier	350	250	8	300	150	
Corsair	150	100	2	100	80	
Dark Archon	250	200	4	25	200	
Dark Templar	125	100	2	80	40	
Dragoon	125	50	2	100	80	
High Templar	50	150	2	40	40	
Observer	25	75	1	40	20	
Photon Cannon	150	0	0	100	100	
Probe	50	0	1	20	20	
Reaver	200	100	4	100	80	
Scout	300	150	3	150	100	
Shuttle	200	0	2	80	60	
Zealot	100	0	2	80	80	

Terran Unit Table

Unit Name	Minerals	Vespene Gas	Supply	Hit Points	Shield	Ar
Battlecruiser	400	300	8	500	0	
Dropship	100	100	2	150	0	
Firebat	50	25	1	50	0	
Ghost	25	75	1	45	0	
Goliath	100	50	2	125	0	
Marine	50	0	1	40	0	
Medic	50	25	1	60	0	
Missile Turret	100	0	0	200	0	
Science Vessel	100	225	2	200	0	
SCV	50	0	1	60	0	
Siege Tank—Siege	150	100	2	150	0	
Siege Tank—Tank	150	100	2	150	0	
Valkyrie	250	125	3	200	0	
Vulture	75	0	2	80	0	
Wraith	150	100	2	120	0	

OUND ATTACK	AIR ATTACK	AIR\GROUND ATTACK MODIFIER	SPLASH DAMAGE	BUILD TIME
10	10	1	NO	160
30	30	3	YES	20
6	6	1	NO	140
0	5	1	YES	40
0	0	0	NO	20
40	0	3	NO	50
20	20	2	NO	40
0	0	0	NO	50
0	0	0	NO	40
20	20	0	NO	50
5	5	0	NO	20
100	0	0	YES	70
8	28	2\1	NO	80
0	0	0	NO	60
16	0	2	NO	40

OUND ATTACK	AIR ATTACK	AIR\GROUND ATTACK MODIFIER	SPLASH DAMAGE	BUILD TIME
25	25	3	NO	160
0	0	0	NO	50
16	0	2	YES	24
10	10	1	NO	50
12	20	4\1	NO	40
6	6	1	NO	24
0	0	0	NO	30
0	20	0	NO	30
0	0	0	NO	80
5	0	0	NO	20
70	0	5	YES	50
30	0	3	NO	50
0	5	1	YES	60
20	0	2	NO	30
8	20	1	NO	60

ZERG UNIT TABLE

UNIT NAME	MINERALS	VESPENE GAS	SUPPLY	HIT POINTS	SHIELD	ARMO
Broodling	0	0	0	30	0	0
Defiler	50	150	2	80	0	1
Devourer	250	150	2	250	0	2
Drone	50	0	1	40	0	0
Egg	0	0	0	200	0	10
Guardian	150	200	2	150	0	2
Hydralisk	75	25	1	80	0	0
Infested Terran	100	50	1	60	0	0
Larva	0	0	0	25	0	10
Lurker	125	125	2	125	0	1
Mutalisk	100	100	2	120	0	0
Overlord	100	0	0	200	0	0
Queen	100	150	2	120	0	0
Scourge	12	38	0.5	25	0	0
Spore Colony	175	0	0	400	0	0
Sunken Colony	175	0	0	400	0	0
Ultralisk	200	200	6	400	0	1
Zergling	25	0	0.5	35	0	0

PROTOSS STRUCTURES

PROTOSS STRUCTURE	MINERALS NEEDED TO BUILD	VESPENE NEEDED TO BUILD
Gateway	150	0
Forge	200	0
Cybernetics	200	0
Shield Battery	100	0
Robotics Facility	200	200
Stargate	200	200
Citadel of Adun	200	100
Robotics Support Bay	50	100
Observatory	150	100
Fleet Beacon	300	200
Templar Archives	100	200
Arbiter Tribunal	200	150
Nexus	400	0
Pylon	100	0
Assimilator	100	0

OUND ATTACK	AIR ATTACK	ATTACK MODIFIER	SPLASH DAMAGE	BUILD TIME
4	0	1	NO	0
0	0	0	NO	50
0	25	2	Special	40
5	0	0	NO	20
0	0	0	NO	0
20	0	2	NO	40
10	10	1	NO	28
500	0	0	YES	40
0	0	0	NO	0
20	0	2	YES	40
9	9	1	NO	40
0	0	0	NO	40
0	0	0	NO	50
0	110	0	NO	30
0	15	0	NO	20
40	0	0	NO	20
20	0	3	NO	60
5	0	1	NO	28

SHIELD	HIT POINTS	BUILD TIME
500	500	60
550	550	40
500	500	60
200	200	30
500	500	80
600	600	70
450	450	60
450	450	30
250	250	30
500	500	60
500	500	60
500	500	60
750	750	120
300	300	30
450	450	40

Terran Structures

TERRAN STRUCTURE	MINERALS NEEDED TO BUILD	VESPENE NEEDED TO BUILD
Command Center	400	0
Supply Depot	100	0
Refinery	100	0
Barracks	150	0
Engineering Bay	125	0
Academy	200	0
Bunker	100	0
Factory	200	100
Armory	100	50
Starport	150	100
Science Facility	150	200
Machine Shop	50	50
Control Tower	50	50
Physics Lab	50	50
Covert Operations	50	50
Nuclear Silo	100	100
Comsat Station	50	50

Zerg Structures

ZERG STRUCTURE	MINERALS NEEDED TO BUILD	VESPENE NEEDED TO BUILD
Hatchery	300	0
Creep Colony	75	0
Extractor	50	0
Spawning Pool	150	0
Evolution Chamber	75	0
Hydralisk Den	100	50
Spire	200	150
Queen's Nest	150	100
Nydus Canal	150	0
Ultralisk Cavern	150	200
Defiler Mound	100	100
Greater Spire	100	150
Lair	150	100
Hive	200	150

SHIELD	HIT POINTS	BUILD TIME
0	1,500	120
0	500	40
0	750	40
0	1,000	80
0	850	60
0	600	80
0	350	30
0	1,250	80
0	750	80
0	1,300	70
0	850	80
0	750	40
0	500	40
0	600	40
0	750	40
0	600	80
0	500	40

SHIELD	HIT POINTS	BUILD TIME
0	1,250	120
0	400	20
0	750	40
0	750	80
0	750	40
0	850	40
0	600	120
0	850	60
0	250	40
0	600	80
0	850	60
0	1,000	120
0	1,800	100
0	2,500	120

Appendix B: Counter List

TERRAN UNIT	TERRAN COUNTER	PROTOSS COUNTER	ZERG COUNTER
Marine	Firebat/Vulture	Zealot/Reaver	Lurker/Guardian
Firebat	Siege Tank/Goliath	Dragoon/Reaver	Hydralisk
Ghost	Vulture/Science Vessel	Zealot	Hydralisk
Vulture	Siege Tank	Dragoon	Hydralisk
Siege Tank	Wraith	Scout	Mutalisk
Goliath	Siege Tank	Dragoon	Hydralisk
Wraith	Valkyrie	Corsair	Mutalisk/Devourer
Battlecruiser	Wraith	Scout	Devourer
Science Vessel	Wraith	Scout	Mutalisk
Valkyrie	Battlecruiser	Carrier	Devourer
Medic	Science Vessel	Reaver	Queen

PROTOSS UNIT	TERRAN COUNTER	PROTOSS COUNTER	ZERG COUNTER
Zealot	Firebat/Vulture	Reaver	Lurker
Dragoon	Siege Tank	Dragoon/Reaver	Zergling
Templar	Science Vessel	Arbiter	Queen
Archon	Siege Tank	Reaver	Hydralisk
Reaver	Wraith/Siege Tank	Scout	Mutalisk
Scout	Valkyrie	Corsair	Mutalisk/Devourer
Corsair	Battlecruiser	Carrier	Mutalisk/Devourer
Carrier	Wraith	Scout	Devourer/Scourge
Arbiter	Science Vessel	Scout	Scourge

ZERG UNIT	TERRAN COUNTER	PROTOSS COUNTER	ZERG COUNTER
Zergling	Firebat/Vulture	Zealot/Reaver	Lurker
Hydralisk	Marine/Siege Tank	Reaver	Zergling
Ultralisk	Siege Tank	Archon	Queen
Mutalisk	Valkyrie	Corsair	Mutalisk/Devourer
Guardian	Wraith	Scout	Mutalisk/Devourer
Devourer	Wraith	Scout	Mutalisk/Scourge
Scourge	Battlecruiser	Corsair	Mutalisk
Lurker	Siege Tank	Reaver	Guardian
Queen	Science Vessel/Medic	Corsair	Scourge
Defiler	Science Vessel/Medic	Zealot	Lurker

Appendix C: Unit and Building Dependency Charts

Probe
| ▷ Nexus |

Zealot
| Nexus |
| ▷ Gateway |

Dragoon
| Nexus |
| ▷ Gateway |
| Cybernetics Core |

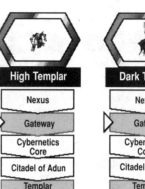

High Templar
| Nexus |
| ▷ Gateway |
| Cybernetics Core |
| Citadel of Adun |
| Templar Archives |

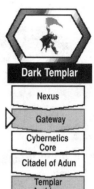

Dark Templar
| Nexus |
| ▷ Gateway |
| Cybernetics Core |
| Citadel of Adun |
| Templar Archives |

Protoss

Unit Dependencies

 unit produced at

 unit requires

parent unit requires

Shuttle
| Nexus |
| Gateway |
| Cybernetics Core |
| ▷ Robotics Facility |

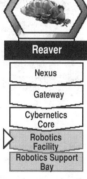

Reaver
| Nexus |
| Gateway |
| Cybernetics Core |
| ▷ Robotics Facility |
| Robotics Support Bay |

Observer
| Nexus |
| Gateway |
| Cybernetics Core |
| ▷ Robotics Facility |
| Observatory |

Scout
| Nexus |
| Gateway |
| Cybernetics Core |
| ▷ Stargate |

Corsair
| Nexus |
| Gateway |
| Cybernetics Core |
| ▷ Stargate |

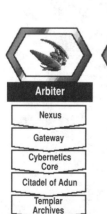

Arbiter
| Nexus |
| Gateway |
| Cybernetics Core |
| Citadel of Adun |
| Templar Archives |
| ▷ Stargate |
| Arbiter Tribunal |

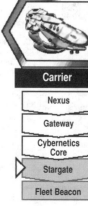

Carrier
| Nexus |
| Gateway |
| Cybernetics Core |
| ▷ Stargate |
| Fleet Beacon |

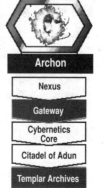

Archon
| Nexus |
| Gateway |
| Cybernetics Core |
| Citadel of Adun |
| Templar Archives |
| ▷ Merge Two High Templars |

Dark Archon
| Nexus |
| Gateway |
| Cybernetics Core |
| Citadel of Adun |
| Templar Archives |
| ▷ Merge Two Dark Templars |

Terran

Unit Dependencies

SCV
- Command Center ▷

Marine
- Command Center
- Barracks ▷

Firebat
- Command Center
- Barracks ▷
- Academy

Medic
- Command Center
- Barracks ▷
- Academy

Ghost
- Command Center
- Barracks ▷
- Academy
- Factory
- Starport
- Science Facility
- Covert Ops

Vulture
- Command Center
- Barracks
- Factory ▷

Siege Tank
- Command Center
- Barracks
- Factory ▷
- Machine Shop

Goliath
- Command Center
- Barracks
- Factory ▷
- Armory

Wraith
- Command Center
- Barracks
- Factory
- Starport ▷

Observer
- Command Center
- Barracks
- Factory
- Starport ▷
- Control Tower

Science Vessel
- Command Center
- Barracks
- Factory
- Starport ▷
- Control Tower
- Science Facility

Valkyrie Frigate
- Command Center
- Barracks
- Factory
- Starport ▷
- Control Tower
- Armory

Battlecruiser
- Command Center
- Barracks
- Factory
- Starport ▷
- Control Tower
- Science Facility
- Physics Lab

Legend:
- ▷ unit produced at
- unit requires
- parent unit requires

Zerg

Unit Dependencies

Overlord

- Hatchery

Drone

- Hatchery

Zergling

- Hatchery
- Spawning Pool

Hydralisk

- Hatchery
- Spawning Pool
- Hydralisk Den

Lurker

- Hatchery
- Spawning Pool
- Hydralisk Den
- Upgrade to Lair
- Evolve Lurker Aspect
- ▷ Morph from Hydralisk

Scourge

- Hatchery
- Spawning Pool
- Upgrade to Lair
- Spire

Mutalisk

- Hatchery
- Spawning Pool
- Upgrade to Lair
- Spire

Guardian

- Hatchery
- Spawning Pool
- Upgrade to Lair
- Spire
- Queeen's Nest
- Upgrade to Hive
- Greater Spire
- ▷ Morph from Mutalisk

Devourer

- Hatchery
- Spawning Pool
- Upgrade to Lair
- Spire
- Queeen's Nest
- Upgrade to Hive
- Greater Spire
- ▷ Morph from Mutalisk

Queen

- Hatchery
- Spawning Pool
- Upgrade to Lair
- Queeen's Nest

Ultralisk
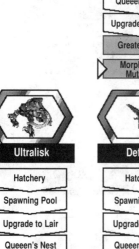
- Hatchery
- Spawning Pool
- Upgrade to Lair
- Queeen's Nest
- Upgrade to Hive
- Ultralisk Cavern

Defiler

- Hatchery
- Spawning Pool
- Upgrade to Lair
- Queeen's Nest
- Upgrade to Hive
- Defiler Mound

Infested Terran

- Hatchery
- Spawning Pool
- Upgrade to Lair
- Queeen's Nest
- ▷ Infested Command Center

- ▷ unit produced at
- unit requires
- parent unit requires

247

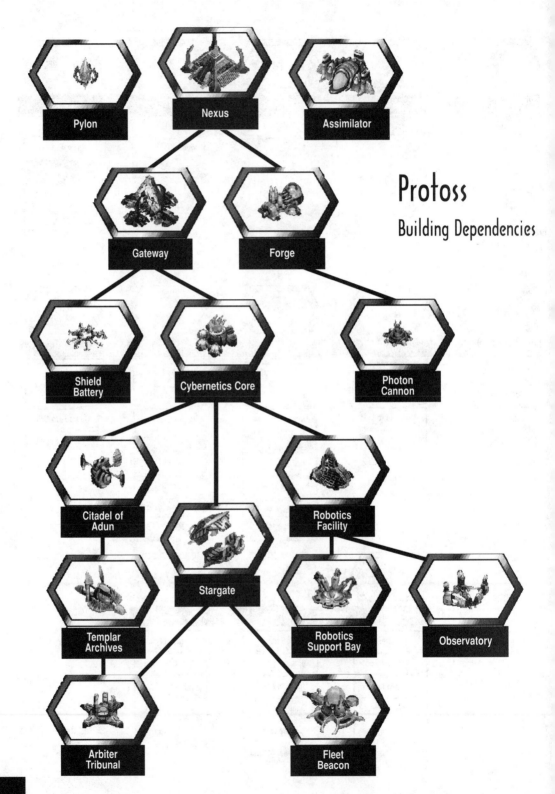

Pylon

Nexus

Assimilator

Protoss

Building Dependencies

Gateway

Forge

Shield Battery

Cybernetics Core

Photon Cannon

Citadel of Adun

Robotics Facility

Stargate

Templar Archives

Robotics Support Bay

Observatory

Arbiter Tribunal

Fleet Beacon

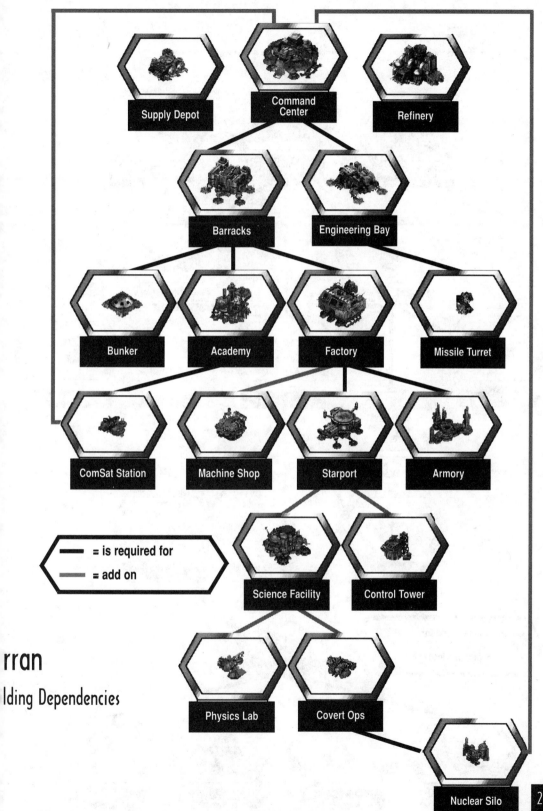

Supply Depot

Command Center

Refinery

Barracks

Engineering Bay

Bunker

Academy

Factory

Missile Turret

ComSat Station

Machine Shop

Starport

Armory

Science Facility

Control Tower

= is required for

= add on

Physics Lab

Covert Ops

Nuclear Silo

rran

lding Dependencies

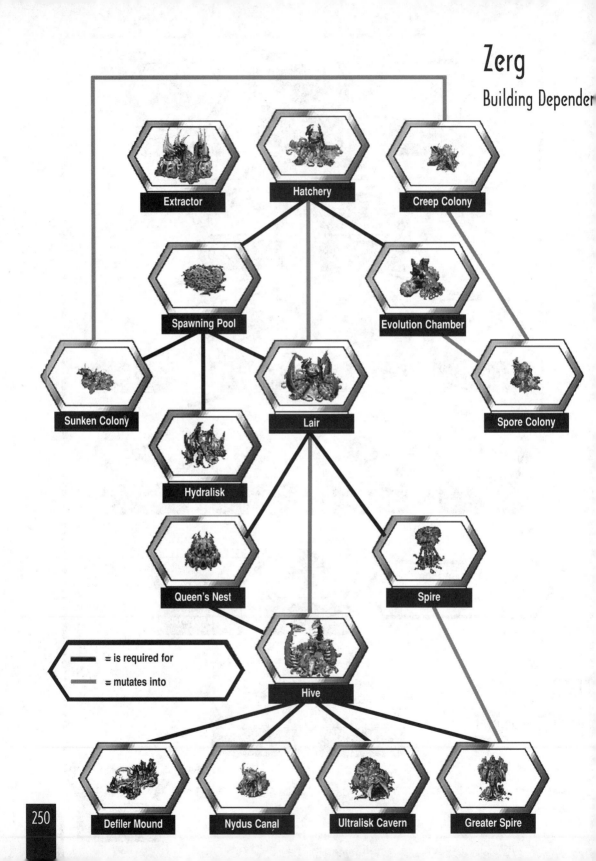

Appendix D: *Starcraft: Brood War* Cheat Codes

As in the original *Starcraft* (and *Warcraft* and *Warcraft II* before it), *Brood War* does allow you certain latitudes when it comes to cheating. In fact, you have the same power over *Brood War*'s units that you had in the original *Starcraft*. You can build faster, get resources, move from level to level, view cinematic sequences, and even build the entire tech tree in the blink of an eye.

I give you these cheats with this warning: don't use them until *after* you've finished the game on your own. If you use the cheats to help you win certain missions, you'll only be denying yourself the real fun of the game. Besides, a level won with cheats won't let you proceed to the next level (unless you cheat to get there).

At any rate, these cheats can provide their own kind of fun, so whenever you choose to use them, enjoy them.

To enable cheats from inside the game, press Enter, type in the cheat code, and then press Enter again.

Instantly win current level:	there is no cow level
Instantly lose current level:	game over man
All units are invincible:	power overwhelming
Receive 10,000 Minerals/Gas:	show me the money
Receive 10,000 Minerals:	whats mine is mine
Receive 10,000 Gas:	breathe deep
Free Upgrades to all units:	something for nothing
Reveal entire map:	black sheep wall
Fast Build Mode:	operation cwal
Disable Level Victory:	staying alive
Free Technology Upgrades:	medieval man
Disable Tech Tree:	modify the phase variance
Disable Food/Psi Requirements:	food for thought
Infinite Energy:	the gathering
Disable persistent Fog of War:	war aint what it used to be
Play Secret Zerg Song:	radio free zerg (this cheat available only when playing as Zerg)
Enable level skipping:	ophelia
After enabling level skipping, from inside game:	(press Enter, type in the level you want to jump to, and then press Enter again)

Starcraft Missions

When using the level skip code, type "ophelia" and then hit Enter. Then type the mission number (see examples below).

terran1, terran2, etc.
zerg1, zerg2, etc.
protoss1, protoss2, etc.

Starcraft: Brood War Missions

For *Starcraft: Brood War* missions, you must type 'x' before the mission number (see examples below).

xterran1, xterran2, etc.
xzerg1, xzerg2, etc.
xprotoss1, xprotoss2, etc.

JUST WHEN YOU THOUGHT IT WAS SAFE TO GO BACK INTO HELL...
DIABLO II™
COMING FOR 1999
VISIT BLIZZARD'S WEBSITE AT WWW.BLIZZARD.COM
BLIZZARD ENTERTAINMENT